# YouGPT Before ChatGPT

How To Implement Human-Centered AI That Improves Decision-Making, Uncovers Hidden Opportunities, And Scales Revenue

JOACHIM LÉPINE, M. ED.

The author would like to express sincere gratitude to Michelle Kulp, book coach, for her invaluable support; to Roberta Weir, editor, for her meticulous work in refining this manuscript; and to Ann Marie Boulanger, for her final revision.

Special thanks also to Zeljka Vukojivić for the beautiful cover design, Jessica Andersen for strategic guidance, Garen Bell for helpful feedback, and Veronica Goldspiel for formatting assistance.

Contact us at info@joachimlepine.com

First Kindle edition, 2026

ISBN: 978-1-0695192-3-8 (Kindle)

978-1-0695192-4-5 (paperback)

978-1-0695192-5-2 (hardcover)

# Unlock exclusive bonus training

Get the YouGPT Before ChatGPT Mini-Course

Visit: ***www.yougptbook.com***

Or scan the QR code below:

# Contents

# Foreword

There are moments in your career where you come across people who don't just consume information—they deeply understand it. They interpret it, break it down into simple, digestible "brain nuggets," and then do something even more powerful: They use it to teach, to help, and to inspire others.

And every once in a while, if you're lucky, those people become more than just colleagues. They become friends—the kind who challenge your thinking, raise your standards, and then go off and do something big that makes you smile, pause, and say... job well done.

And then, if you're even luckier, they ask you to write the foreword to their super awesome book.

This is one of those moments.

I've had the opportunity to work closely with the author behind YouGPT for a number of years, and what stood out to me early on wasn't just curiosity—it was intent. The kind of intent that leads someone to infuse their soul into every word that they write. Someone who sees past the fear of, "This tool is the end of our industry," and instead asks, "What can I become if I use it strategically?" That question alone already changes the outcome of what may have been.

Needless to say, we are living through one of the most important shifts in modern history. Not because of artificial intelligence itself, but because of what it reveals about us—about who we are.

For the first time, access to intelligence is no longer the constraint. The real constraint is how we think, how we ask, how we decide, and how we act.

In other words, the differentiator is no longer the tool. It's you—and that is wholly motivating and terrifying. We are, in many ways, our own limit.

That's what makes this book different.

YouGPT is not about learning prompts, shortcuts, hacks, or surface-level productivity gains. It's about something much deeper—and far more valuable. It's about developing a way of thinking that allows you to partner with intelligence rather than passively consume it.

Because here's the truth: Most people will use AI to do things faster. Very few will use it to rewire their thought process and perspective, and, in doing so, better themselves. And that gap is where the difference lies.

What this book does exceptionally well is bring that realization down to earth. It takes something that can feel abstract, overwhelming, even intimidating, and turns it into something practical—something usable, something you can apply the moment you put it down. And that matters.

Because the real value of AI is not in what it can do—although that's pretty cool, too. It's in what it enables you to do.

The title YouGPT is not accidental. It's a reminder that the quality of what you get out of these tools is directly tied to the quality of what you bring into them: your clarity, your curiosity, your discipline, and your willingness to iterate, refine, and challenge your own assumptions—and your habits.

AI was never intended to be a passive experience. It's an active one. And if you approach this book with the right mindset, it will do more than teach you how to use AI... it will change how you approach problems, decisions, and opportunities moving forward.

So, as you read this, I'd encourage you to do one thing: Apply it wholeheartedly. Because the value of this book will not come from the pages themselves, but from what you choose to do with them.

We are entering a time where the chasm between those who use AI and those who leverage it will widen quickly. The ones who win will not be the ones with the most *access* to AI, but the ones with the most *intention*.

This book is a guiding light in that direction. And if you look past the pages, the author of *YouGPT* may very well change the way you think—not just about AI, but about yourself.

Remember: The future isn't about AI replacing you. It's about you becoming infinitely better than yesterday... becoming empowered through intention.

There it is.

— Bryan Montpetit

# Introduction

***"AI is the new electricity."***

-Andrew Ng, *Co-founder of Google Brain*

## "Let's ask ChatGPT!"

Sitting pensively in my living room on a chilly November day, holding my cell phone while gazing out at the snow-covered yard, I confided to my friend, "Hey, I've been thinking about doing an executive certificate at MIT. I'd love to get your opinion. Do you think it's a good idea?"

His answer was nearly instantaneous: "I dunno. Let's ask ChatGPT!"

I was floored.

I didn't want ChatGPT's opinion. I wanted my friend's point of view, professional judgment, and honest, critical, potentially brutal feedback. I wanted him to push back if my idea was hare-brained and ill-considered.

What I did not want was a robotic "yes-man."

Yet, increasingly, in small, everyday moments like these, under the spell of humanlike generative AI, we are beginning to turn to machines—delegating our thinking, intuition, relationships, creativity, and decision-making to them.

Kids are growing up using AI-powered apps and games. Some teens have romantic AI partners (yes, really). Adults are asking AI to write emails and make their decisions. All of this with precious few guidelines or guardrails.

But is this what we really want?

By now, we've all seen the ads plastered across social media:

*"Let AI do it for you."*

*"Fire your copywriter and use this chatbot instead."*

*"Write your blog post in a single click."*

*"With our new app, you'll never need to create anything again."*

*"Get instant career advice without having to talk to anyone."*

*"Use our AI bot and then clean up the draft so it sounds like you wrote it."*

But if you're like me, you feel a deep sense of unease in your gut when you come across these messages.

Everywhere we turn, our new AI-driven environment prioritizes speed, efficiency, instantaneity, and, above all, outsourcing our brains to artificial intelligence—as if it were a given that these are the only things we value in our lives and work.

And when we stop and think about it, this messaging makes perfect sense. Ever since ChatGPT burst onto the world stage in November 2022, developers of AI-powered apps have had a vested interest in reiterating that AI is a silver bullet with nothing but advantages for humanity.

Occam's razor applies here: The reason for this message is simple and obvious. AI companies stand to profit if we use their tools frequently. For example, Statista projects the AI industry will be worth up to $1.2 trillion by 2030.[1]

---

1. Statista, *The AI Market Is Poised for Explosive Growth*, 2025.

As people and companies increasingly incorporate AI into their daily habits, the economic value to AI companies is poised to balloon dramatically.

## People are using AI incorrectly

Thoughtless use of AI also raises an interesting conundrum: Because of the "one-click everything" mindset, many people today are misusing AI.

It's treated like a slot machine. We feed it and hope we'll "win" the right answer. And sometimes we do! Today's large language models (LLMs) have an uncanny ability to tell us what we want to hear and sometimes provide useful information. And the fact that the answers aren't always right only makes it more addictive. Like a Las Vegas slot machine or social media, it gives us intermittent rewards, in other words, endless dopamine hits.

Except when we relinquish our own potential for a chance to win a "sometimes useful" answer from AI, the trade-off isn't exactly in our favor. We often end up overestimating the quality of what we've produced.

In short, the problem we're seeing today is twofold. First, by using AI uncritically, we risk turning our brains to mush and abdicating the best of what makes us human. And second, most of us are using AI incorrectly, treating it like a slot machine. The result? Unusable slop.

## Introducing a new paradigm: YouGPT Before ChatGPT

This book suggests a simple way to fix both problems.

You are going to learn a more strategic way to tap into your unlimited potential, respond constructively to AI, improve your life, and build a better business, whether you're an employee or a business owner.

You are going to learn how to use "YouGPT" before ChatGPT.

## Who am I? Why listen to me?

My name is Joe, and I am proud to have built two successful companies (a service business and an online academy) in the professional field Microsoft considers the most AI-applicable and therefore replaceable on the planet: language translation.[2]

I began as a professional French-to-English translator in the 2000s. I worked with prestigious clients worldwide, taught university courses in my field for 15 years, and then cofounded a professional development platform to help translators thrive in the age of AI.

Over the past 20 years, I've hired business coaches to help me grow and mature as a business owner, build trust with clients in a competitive field, scale successfully, make better decisions, forge partnerships, help people more effectively, and create a flourishing career.

More recently, after leading countless workshops on business and tech topics for thousands of professionals worldwide, I've increasingly been called upon as an AI and strategic advisor. Over the years, I've provided training and consulting for organizations including NATO, Gowling, PwC, the UN, and many others. They come to me for advice and training on human-first workflows, AI integration, and conveying our value effectively in the AI era.

In other words, I help experts and teams build thriving businesses and organizations, not by outsourcing their brains to AI, but by adopting human-first frameworks, trust-building strategies, marketing engines, and workflows.

Putting people first is always my goal. My experience has been that when we do so, whether in our decision-making or our (sometimes AI-augmented) workflows, the results are spectacular. And it just feels better.

---

2. Preston Fore, Fortune.com, *Microsoft researchers have revealed the 40 jobs most exposed to AI—and even teachers make the list*, 2026.

In my own business, I tap into my intuition to come up with ideas, and only then do I use technology to augment what I create, add value, and make the content more accessible to a broader audience.

This book is a good example. I used advanced journaling techniques (which you will learn in this book) to dig deep, leverage my intuition, draw on insightful conversations and anecdotes, and refine my ideas. Then I used AI to transcribe the text, organize my ideas into buckets, separate sentences into paragraphs, and conduct keyword research to help me publish in the right categories. I still hired humans for everything from cover design to editing, because I care about quality.

The process has been enjoyable and rewarding. It's the exact opposite of what I see many "AI guru authors" peddling today, namely, having AI write your book for you.

That's just one of many down-to-earth examples you'll find in this book. There are so many inspiring ways to reinvigorate our humanity, using AI and technology the right way—not as a crutch, but as jet propulsion on our terms.

I'm very proud of this testimonial from a corporate training client: "Instead of worrying and stressing out about the change AI is ushering into our organization, now I know that machines can be valuable partners and that they can stimulate our creativity."

That's exactly what I love to hear. It's why I'm passionate about working with business owners and organizations to help them use AI ethically and effectively in ways that align with their core values.

## Your most valuable asset is you

One thing we can be thankful for in the AI era, even for the AI-averse, is that artificial intelligence is showing us how important our humanity, connection, and decision-making really are.

We are relearning the importance of critical thinking, relationships, and flipping on our personal "creator switch," whether as entrepreneurs or intrapreneurs. And the very limitations of AI are helping us understand what only we can bring to the table to create "Aligned and Integral" (AI) businesses and organizations.

By the end of this book, you will master amazing yet little-known techniques that will help you make the most of your most valuable asset: you. And as a happy by-product, you'll learn how to use AI the right way, i.e., not like a slot machine but as a propulsion mechanism that can take you to undreamed-of heights, but only if and when you choose to use it.

Always remember, YOU are the pilot in the cockpit. AI can be a helpful copilot, but it needs to be used carefully, and only when it makes sense.

Don't let AI run the show. And don't let anyone tell you otherwise.

When you turn the page, you're going to find out why.

# Chapter One

# The Velvet Sundown of Humanity

***"Technology is nothing. What's important is that you have faith in people, that they're basically good and smart, and if you give them tools, they'll do wonderful things with them."***

-Steve Jobs, Co-founder of Apple

Have you heard of The Velvet Sundown, the 70s-style alt-rock band that went viral on Spotify in 2025?

Despite music critics calling it generic and lacking soul, the album managed to rack up over one million monthly listeners on Spotify before it was revealed as a "synthetic music project."[1] In other words, the band and its music were AI-generated.

There are several interesting aspects to explore here.

One of them is that, after being trained on a lot of music—whether legally or otherwise—artificial intelligence was used to produce humanlike content.

This is what generative AI does.

1. David Renshaw, Fader, *The Velvet Sundown's AI saga is 2025's weirdest music story*, 2025.

It generates output that mimics what humans create. We need to keep this distinction top of mind whenever we talk about or use it.

In this case, convincing AI-generated music and even album covers. Some people actually enjoyed the music, even though it lacked uniqueness. It was more of a mishmash of laid-back 70s pop.

Generative pre-trained transformers (GPTs) are trained on massive datasets, including text, images, music, and audio. This is considered legal (although many disagree) because, according to AI companies, the training falls under fair use.[2]

In other words, AI generates something new rather than simply copying and regurgitating it. GenAI is a recombination mechanism that uses probabilistic modeling and intentional, "controlled" chaos. This is also why, if you enter the same prompt twice, it will often give you two different answers.

After some time, The Velvet Sundown's fans noticed some irregularities: an album cover where a microphone could be seen disappearing into the singer's arm, and the guitarist's fingers appearing to be fused.[3]

Yet AI pulled off quite a feat. The Velvet Sundown sounded human enough to pass a sort of "musical Turing test." People interacted with the music and found it convincingly humanlike.

It was an intentional hoax that has sparked considerable reflection on AI, copyright, attribution, and the very nature of creativity itself.

For this book, let's focus on the generic dimension of the music created.

---

2. Katherine Klosek, Association of Research Libraries, *Training Generative AI Models on Copyrighted Works Is Fair Use*, 2024.

3. Caitlin McCormack, NY Post, *Rock band with more than 1 million Spotify listeners reveals it's entirely AI-generated — down to the musicians themselves*, 2025.

Today, anyone can access music-, image-, and text-generating apps. But when everyone has access to the same AI apps, AI ceases to be a differentiating factor.

To transpose this to the business world, AI may become an operational baseline. Still, without thoughtful frameworks and meaningful human contribution, it's unlikely to confer a competitive advantage in and of itself.

This becomes glaringly obvious when generative AI is used to develop a business strategy. For example, if you ask a bot to write a business plan, the result will tend to be eye-rollingly generic and insufficiently tailored to be of any use.

The output can be improved with higher-quality, higher-quantity input. After all, garbage in, garbage out, and quality in, quality out.

Yet at the end of the day, no matter how many times I've asked an AI to generate a one-page business plan, it doesn't hold a candle to working with a business coach who asks difficult questions and dares to push back instead of being a yes-man.

The same phenomenon was alluded to in a recent MIT Sloan article titled *"Why AI Will Not Provide Sustained Competitive Advantage."*[4] The article is neither for nor against AI; it merely points out that when everyone has access to a tool, that tool ceases to be an advantage in itself.

Instead, according to the article, the future drivers of success will likely remain passion and innovation. In other words, the human factor.

And yes, AI bots can be trained to mimic people and deliver increasingly tailored outputs. However, slop is slop, and most of us still know it when we see it. We feel it too, whether we're on the creating or consuming end.

---

4. David Wingate, Barclay L. Burns, and Jay B. Barney, MIT Sloan Management Review, *Why AI Will Not Provide Sustainable Competitive Advantage*, 2025.

## Transposing music to business

You may be wondering whether a parallel can really be drawn between music and business strategy. It depends. If the goal is to whip up something that sounds convincingly humanlike, generative AI will deliver.

However, AI is not the first place to go to forge a vision of the future, question deep values, and ensure alignment and integrity.

For these critical functions, it's better to start with a gut check before turning to AI to consider the details. When we start by prompting our own minds, the input tends to be of much higher quality and will usually produce better output—by orders of magnitude.

## Human and AI value propositions: a lesson from hypnotherapy

Technology can certainly be useful as a complement.

Here's an example from a different field: I have gone to a wonderful hypnotherapist who has helped me with my public speaking and overcoming some trauma from my youth.

We have done deep and transformative work together, and the therapy has been profound and more than worthwhile.

After starting the treatment, I also bought a hypnosis app that I can turn to for instant hypnosis. It's quite handy since I can't contact my hypnotherapist in the middle of the night when I can't sleep, or when I want a quick rest and recharge with a midday nap. (Okay, technically, I could try calling her, but I don't think she would appreciate it!)

To me, they each play fundamentally different roles. I turn to the professional hypnotherapist for deep healing to achieve a big, important outcome. I use the app for quick maintenance support at any time.

The app I use (Harmony) is not specifically AI, but it could have been. For example, AI-generated hypnosis tracks abound on YouTube and are fast becoming indistinguishable from human-created tracks. The same is true of talking-head videos and many other things.

Circling back to The Velvet Sundown, while the AI music is humanlike, it's no replacement for real music made by real people.

## Who's training who?

Consider this: If we take AI use one step too far and have it create everything in our stead, there is a real danger that, instead of molding the machine, we will end up being molded by it.

Traditionally, humans believe that we program machines, and we have transferred this logic to AI, thinking we've programmed it, and it's been trained. After all, GPT stands for generative pre-trained transformer.

But what if it's really training us?

When we think we're merely "checking the AI output" to tweak it to our liking, isn't it likely that our tastes, even our thought processes and decisions, are being shaped by the machine instead of our humanity? And imagine how deeply AI will alter our thinking in a few short years when this technology generates inconceivable amounts of content that we are exposed to at nearly every turn.

## About words and intent

Bear with me: We're going to get a bit woo-woo here.

When I receive important emails from coaching and consulting clients, I can apply a generic AI response with a single click. In the best-case scenario, this might save me a few seconds.

Except I believe there is power and intent behind my words.

When I write emails, I write every word myself, and I mean every word. To me, there's a difference. Regardless of how the message is interpreted, I want my intent and my soul to be infused into every line, in keeping with my personal AI (Alignment and Integrity).

This is also why I don't use AI to create generic output for social media or my newsletter. When I sit down and put love, power, care, and vulnerability into my content, however imperfect it may be, it resonates much more deeply with people. And the success of my humble online academy suggests I'm on to something.

I know all this could be data fed into a custom GPT, and many experts and professionals are going this route today. However, the thought leaders and companies I follow proudly create their own content. I know when I read their words, I'm getting real value, because AI didn't write it. AI merely predicts the next likely word in a string of text based on pattern recognition, however advanced it may be.

In other words, maybe output isn't the only important consideration when we use AI.

The intent behind what I create matters to me. I would rather write an imperfect post from my heart and soul than click once to churn out generic content that may or may not deliver the results I want.

Not everyone will agree. But if you picked up this book, the concept likely resonates with you, too.

There are plenty of thoughtful ways to benefit from AI without abdicating our humanity to it.

## The Emoto water crystals

Have you heard of the Emoto water crystal experiments? Masaru Emoto, a Japanese scientist, exposed water to different words and then photographed the ice crystals that formed.

He found that water spoken to with positive intent formed beautiful, unique crystals, whereas water exposed to harsh music or negative words formed fractured, ugly crystals.

Considering that our bodies are mostly water, imagine the impact of a kind, healing word—not just in our brain, but throughout our body. That's why we need to be careful about what we tell children, and indeed, everyone we interact with. Our words and the intent behind them profoundly affect others.

I will concede that Emoto's experiments have been criticized as pseudoscience.[5] And yet, when someone gives us a harsh rebuke versus a kind and supportive word, don't we feel that intent ripple through our being? I certainly do. And I believe that intent matters.

Let's be clear, the idea isn't to say AI should never be used. This book's purpose is not to advocate for or against AI. Instead, I'm suggesting that whether we're reading content from our favorite creator, a book like this one, or an email, the intent behind the words matters.

## Choosing our medium wisely in an AI-saturated world

Taking this one step further, when responding to important emails, I now send a video reply to the person I'm communicating with. I press a button on my video recording app, read over their email, respond in real time, look into the camera, share my honest thoughts, speak from the heart, and click send.

The response from my clients and business partners has been overwhelming. They frequently thank me for taking the time to personalize the interaction, even though it took me less time to record a video than to write or AI-edit an email, especially for a longer or more delicate topic.

5. Wikipedia, *The Hidden Messages in Water*, 2024.

So, even though AI often suggests email messages we can use, it's worth giving some thought to which process and channel best serves our goals.

Personalized video emails have been a game changer for my business. They build trust, multiplying referrals and opportunities with my business partners.

This is the power of putting humans first. The videos I record are not perfect. In fact, I don't want them to be, since imperfection and vulnerability are pillars of trust. They're sent from the heart with intent, and this is so much more powerful than anything AI could cook up for me.

## Why disappointment often follows AI-generated content

I received an email pitch the other day to partner with another business. It started by talking about my own company, which was refreshing. Most email pitches I receive are usually very self-centered and start with something like, "We have 20 years of experience doing XYZ." But this email was specific to my company and what I did, albeit in very odd, generic-sounding terms. Then it offered to partner with me, using lots of em dashes, words like "core" and "realm," and the same ideas repeated across paragraphs, which included absolutely no new meaning.

These are tell-tale signs of AI.

After reading that email, I felt put off, even though it was clear the AI had personalized it for my business. I think it's because there was no humanity behind it—just a gimmick, a ploy to make me feel like I was interacting with another human when I was not.

This also happened once when I was traveling. I had to make a phone call to find the right hotel venue for an event where I was speaking. I thought I was speaking to a customer service representative because the AI over the phone sounded so fluid. But I kept getting the runaround, had to start over, and ultimately didn't get an answer to my specific question.

I suddenly realized I was talking to an AI agent, and I wasn't going to get anywhere. I finally went to a hotel help desk to ask where to go. I got my answer in about 15 seconds.

It's worth taking a moment to unpack why this was a disappointing experience.

It's not only because I didn't get the information I wanted; it's also because I didn't feel listened to.

Later, we will examine how AI can be used strategically. But this lack of intent behind AI's words, no matter how well disguised, frequently creates a sense of frustration that no one is listening and that no one really cares.

## Walk away, dance... or fly?

Seth Godin recently asked an insightful question on his blog: "Walk away or dance?"[6] He was asking whether writers and other professionals today should forgo AI or work alongside it to create their content.

This is a great starting point for discussion. However, binary thinking (i.e., choosing whether or not to use AI) may not be sufficient to address the complex, broader question of how to use AI in society and business today.

After all, when we dance with a partner, we are on equal footing with another human being.

But when it comes to AI, this is not a given. AI is not another human being, with humanity, judgment, intent, and soul.

I like the plane metaphor. We need a pilot in the cockpit who is qualified, trained, and endowed with perception, care, empathy, and professional judgment.

---

6. Seth Godin, Seth's Blog, *Walk away or dance*, 2025.

The pilot may or may not use AI to perform certain operations under the right conditions. Once they have selected the trajectory, i.e., the desired outcome and parameters, they can turn on the booster to activate jet propulsion, if you will.

We are the pilots in the cockpit.

We can choose to use AI or not, to assist us or give us a boost. But AI should not be in control of the plane without our guidance, accountability, and judgment.

Once these criteria are met, we might envision changing course from the "sundown of humanity," or at least the sundown of human creativity and decision-making, to explore more promising skies, on our own terms.

In chapter two, we will look at what this looks like in down-to-earth terms.

## Key Insights

❖ AI imitates, it doesn't originate. It can pass as human but lacks human depth and soul.

❖ AI is a baseline tool. When everyone has access to it, it is no longer a competitive advantage. It's human passion and innovation that drive real advantage.

❖ The better the input, the better the output. Thoughtful human intent and clarity are what make AI useful.

❖ Overusing AI can shape you. Letting AI create everything risks dulling your own thinking and tastes.

❖ The intention behind words matters. Authentic, human-crafted communication resonates; generic AI text does not.

❖ Humans must remain in control. You are the pilot. AI is only an assistant and a jet propulsion system. It doesn't control the plane.

# Chapter Two

# This is Your Brain on AI

***"The heart has its reasons, which reason does not know."***

-Blaise Pascal

As a kid growing up in the suburbs of Philadelphia, I remember seeing a frequent TV commercial that said, "This is your brain... This is your brain on drugs." It featured an off-putting image of a sputtering egg cooking on high heat.

This may happen to our brains if we use AI indiscriminately. Not to mention the damage currently being done to the human collective by social media, instant gratification, and the endless dopamine hits from our myriad screens and devices.

However, this need not be the case. It all depends on how we use the tool.

To get our bearings, let's look at three key distinctions between AI and human intelligence, or HI.

## AI predicts, humans perceive

AI works by predicting the next word in a string of text, or where a piece of an image might belong in a larger dataset, i.e., a ChatGPT-generated image. All this comes down to prediction, which is predicated on complex algorithms, in turn undergirded by statistical models.

Although AI is very impressive and can create increasingly better outputs, at the end of the day, we never really know what we'll get.

This can make AI incredibly useful when we're looking for pattern-driven insights or seeking to round out an initial idea. But it can be problematic if we confuse it with the way humans produce professional output, which is rooted in perception.

Here's a down-to-earth example: Most texts sent to be translated by professional translators tend to contain errors. The author will inadvertently say the opposite of what they meant, or forget a word, or undermine their own argument.

A professional translator will spot these mistakes and ask the author critical questions, often leading to improvements in both the original and the target text.

AI is different. It lacks empathy. It can't put itself in the reader's place and size up a situation. In fact, AI does not understand words per se. Whereas humans think in terms of word associations rooted in perception, experience, and intention, generative AI processes tokens that are converted into words on the screen. It has no direct sensory grounding or subjective understanding; instead, it relies on numeric vectors learned from token sequences.

Many people think empathy is a soft skill: nice to have, but not essential. Yet the empathy that allows a professional to put themselves in their client's or reader's shoes is precisely what enables them to produce something genuinely useful.

This resonates with what Sade-Chantal Mielczarek describes as safeguarding the 3Cs of human work: critical thinking, creativity, and consciousness.[1] In an AI-saturated world, these are the dimensions that need to be preserved and cultivated in order to continue to produce meaningful work.

---

1. Sade-Chantal Mielczarek, *Safeguarding the 3Cs of the Human Mind: Critical Thinking, Creativity, and Consciousness*, 2025.

For example, while AI will interpret an input literally and miss many mistakes, a professional translator or editor will exercise empathy, read between the lines, and add value to their client through advice.

This can be extrapolated to many more professions and contexts. AI might draft a legal contract by predicting the next word most likely to appear, but the attorney will know why a situation calls for a special clause or the addition of a qualifying word.

These are not trifling details. They are the exact reason people turn to professionals rather than AI for mission-critical, image-sensitive, and high-risk projects of all kinds, whether in graphic design, text, code, or anything else. And it's why we must continue to do so.

## AI calculates, humans care

AI is useful for crunching numbers and checking exchange rates on different days to generate a handy list of business deductions and client payments, ready for an accountant to use in a sales tax report. But it will not do those special things that create meaning and grow a relationship-driven business.

The business strategy I preach and practice is rooted in human relationships and real value. For instance, when one of my key clients holds an event, I often attend. Afterward, I might post about it on social media, including a few pictures and tags. Then I'll write to the client to let them know how wonderful their event was, how valuable I found it, and that I'm happy to share it with my circles.

This human connection has become even more powerful since the pandemic, and given the greater social isolation we experience today, as we increasingly live behind screens of all sizes. When clients know I care and that I've taken a few minutes to add significant value to their projects, they notice and become consistent sources of repeat business and referrals.

Building relationships is best left to humans. And personally, I wouldn't want it any other way. After all, relationships are good for business, but they also add meaning to our lives.

As we saw earlier, AI can scour the internet and send a phony email congratulating a potential client. But there's nothing better than the personal attention of connecting with another person meaningfully and authentically. Just one small act like this each week can dramatically boost your business, in virtually any industry.

Very few people do these things. But the payoff is incredible for the nominal amount of time and effort invested. This is real leverage, and it doesn't require any AI, gimmicks, or funnels.

## AI generates output, a professional delivers an outcome

Finally, AI generates sometimes useful output. What professionals do across all fields is create an outcome for their clients.

If you use AI to generate a blueprint of your dream home in the country, you may get an output that's useful... or not. It might help with gisting, dreaming, or coming up with ideas. But before applying for the building permit and getting to work, you'd better consult an architect who can factor in data points AI overlooked. Because AI doesn't live in your area, it doesn't know all the criteria involved and hasn't experienced anything that would preclude certain choices and make others necessary.

This being said, an architect might use AI to support the design process with professional AI-powered software, which raises a very important point.

If a service provider uses AI to add value via faster or better service, is the service worth more or less?

Logically, it's worth more.

If you go to your favorite dental clinic, and they use a new AI-powered machine that lets you receive faster care, will you be charged less? Of course not. They're probably going to charge more, because they are delivering greater value. In fact, the last time I went to my dentist, they had a poster at the entrance showcasing their latest technology and the value it adds.

The knowledge professions shouldn't balk at AI. They can use the same approach. An attorney who drafts with AI doesn't have to be ashamed of using technology, provided it adds value for the client. However, they must remain in total control of it, continuing to reserve professional acts such as providing the client with a binding contract that will hold up in court.

These three distinctions—predicting vs. perceiving, calculating vs. caring, and generating output vs. delivering an outcome—will go a long way toward underscoring professionals' added value. Even so, it's a fact that today, many will need upskilling to augment their capacity and keep up with industry trends.

The "YouGPT Before ChatGPT" framework can help here.

In the end, I always return to my core values: courage, pride, and integrity. I don't have a problem with using technology if it aligns with my values. That said, I don't see a need to justify myself or provide each client with a 20-page AI-usage policy. Today, using AI in some way, shape, or form is expected in all fields, from car mechanics to doctors to taxi drivers.

Change is the one constant in life, and AI is part of the change we're seeing today.

However, the value of people should never be diminished or perceived as less because they use a tool that provides greater value and requires an investment on the professional's part.

Remember, a bot lets you chat with a generative pre-trained transformer.

But here's what you can do with YouGPT: Give it your Personal Touch.

## YouGPT: giving it your personal touch

Here's a real-life example.

A major consulting client recently contacted me. Their communications team was being asked by clients to review AI-generated texts almost instantaneously. However, a light review was not appropriate for all the texts they received. They needed a way to demonstrate the value of their work beyond a little AI touch-up. They helped their clients understand that not all AI-generated text can just be given a quick read and published anywhere. Often, the output isn't good enough and needs to be rewritten from scratch.

I asked ChatGPT what it thought about this situation. It suggested mentioning that AI can hallucinate or fabricate content and that this poses risks. Then it followed up by providing a few text categories that might require different levels of editing, from light editing to rewriting.

This answer is logical and predictable, but that isn't what I told my consulting client.

Based on my 10 years of experience helping organizations optimize their workflows, I suggested a different way forward: Give clients a choice.

Here's how it works.

If I tell my nine-year-old son to put his jacket on when it's cold, he's going to resist. Trying to persuade human beings to do something, especially something they don't feel like doing, is an uphill battle. We see this in children all the time.

A clever parent will instead carefully offer their child choices.

For example, I can tell my son, "Would you like to wear your jacket or your thick sweater?" He may hesitate for a moment, then he'll grab the sweater, put it on, and rush out the door.

This is a win for me. Not only has he done exactly what I wanted him to do—put on warm clothes so he doesn't catch a cold—but I didn't need to raise my voice or resort to threats, explanations, arguments, or even incentives.

I offered a choice. When my son chose the sweater, he did it joyfully. He felt empowered because it was his decision, not mine.

This is how professionals and teams can negotiate with their clients successfully in the AI era. The key is that it's up to us, as service providers, to reflect on the choices we want to give people. We can leverage mental models and consumer psychology principles to help ensure the outcome we want while maintaining our integrity.

My consulting client was over the moon. I could see a light bulb go on in their minds and their body language shift.

We know that humans are often unreasonable. They don't understand the value of many professionals today. They see ads from tech companies everywhere claiming they can get anything with one click. As a result, professionals can easily feel like they are spending their whole lives on the defensive, fending off the aggression of poorly informed clients.

Offering a thoughtful, curated choice can be a game changer for professionals and teams of all stripes in the AI era, in the context of unreasonable or even insulting requests.

What if my consulting client came to me and I rattled off the generic answer I got from ChatGPT? Do you think they'd have been satisfied? They could have gotten the same answer from any online standard chatbot. They came to me because my unique background in business, AI, and communication has enabled me to build successful businesses in a tough field. I also have a track record of helping others do the same.

This is how I use GPT; it's what I mean when I say, "Giving things my Personal Touch." You can also leverage yours by mining your valuable life experiences for unique insights.

You too have accumulated a treasure trove of wisdom in the course of your life. The key to success is to search within and leverage your life experience and intuition before using AI.

## Key Insights

❖ AI predicts, humans perceive. A professional will sense nuance, errors, and context that AI cannot.

❖ AI calculates, humans care. Real value stems from empathy, trust, and relationships.

❖ AI provides output. Professionals deliver outcomes that work in real life.

❖ Using AI intelligently increases value. Faster, higher-quality service can justify higher fees.

❖ Your advantage is "YouGPT": your personal touch, judgment, and lived experience.

❖ First you, then AI. Use the tool to enhance, not replace, your thinking.

# Chapter Three

# How to Dream, Imagine, and Go the Last Mile

***"Computers are magnificent tools for the realization of our dreams, but no machine can replace the human spark of spirit, compassion, love, and understanding."***

-Louis V. Gerstner Jr., former CEO of IBM

## The last-mile challenge

After publishing my first book, *AI Resilient*, I received a last-minute email from the BBC asking if I would be willing to speak about AI and the future of knowledge professions on their Radio 5 morning show.

I was still high on publishing my first book and thought it would be a wonderful opportunity, so I agreed, even though I'd have to speak at 3:10 a.m. Eastern Time the next day so that people in the UK could tune in live during their morning commute.

I drank lots of coffee and was way too excited on the call, but I survived!

The BBC discussed how, according to PwC's 2025 Global AI Jobs Barometer, many jobs will be lost to AI, but even more jobs will be created by the resulting apps and technologies.[1] It may be a bit early to know whether this will be the case.

What I can say for sure is that my translator coaching clients, who've been willing to learn new things, step out of their comfort zone, take professional development courses, and move up to the premium market in their field, have fared well in the AI era—even in what is considered the most replaceable "text in, text out" field on earth (i.e., language translation).

Part of the reason for their success comes down to what the BBC called the "last-mile challenge." Maybe as AI gets better, it will handle 90% of a job, but humans will provide the critical last 10% that adds irreplaceable value, requiring human judgment, accountability, and decision-making.

I don't know about you, but I'd rather ride with a human cab driver than an empty car with AI at the wheel. I'm also fine with going to see my dentist, who is using a new X-ray machine, but I wouldn't want AI operating a robotic arm to perform my annual cleaning. I want a responsible, perceptive, and intelligent human to handle the last bit of the job.

## Roar of the TAIGR

Here's a case study on how some translators are using AI effectively today. When translating, they are using TAIGR (translation AI contextual groundings retrieval) technology developed by Terminotix.

It allows them to curate their own sets of reliable, professional, human-written texts, then cobble them together into a natural-sounding translation draft using AI in a secure environment.[2]

1. PwC, *The Fearless Future: 2025 Global AI Jobs Barometer*, 2025.

2. Terminotix, *AI translation tailored to your organization*, 2026.

Users can even create their own custom prompts. They can work directly in Microsoft Word, using the prompts they've created, and choose whether to use AI for each sentence.

They can also adjust the "temperature" to make the engine more or less creative, depending on the text type they're working with.

In other words, in this case study, the professional remains in control and is able to ensure an outcome for their client rather than merely generating output.

Like many other AI-augmented workflows, TAIGR is enabling professionals to deliver high-quality work in less time and earn more per hour.

An important caveat is that the professional should always decide whether and how to use AI.

It should not be up to the client, since only the professional can choose the right tool and workflow for the job at hand. That is part of the value they provide.

For instance, it wouldn't be right to draft a website with AI and then ask a graphic designer to clean it up in record time for minimal pay. This would be disrespectful, demeaning, and detrimental to the client's own interests when quality matters.

Instead, people should turn to professionals who use AI to add value and proudly provide their clients with outstanding quality, often in faster turnaround times than before.

In this way, everyone wins.

For this to happen, the service provider must remain in control and possession of the tool; the client must be turned away if they ask the professional to clean up AI slop; and professional associations must stand up for their members and urge them not to charge less because they are using AI.

## Brain atrophy and over-reliance on AI

Several studies have found that outsourcing our brains to AI can dull our critical thinking and creativity.[3] So, let's look at some of the pillars of these two essential factors and how they might intersect and overlap.

## Curiosity and imagination

In large part, creativity comes down to curiosity and imagination. It requires relaxing, putting the mind into an alpha brainwave state, and exploring ideas without predefining the outcome.

It also means imagining new possibilities, a trait that is hard for AI to replicate as a recombining machine.

To tap into our creativity, we need to be willing to learn what imagination really is. Unfortunately, many of us have forgotten how to imagine. Hours of doomscrolling and watching YouTube shorts rather than cultivating this most precious human ability haven't helped.

Albert Einstein is credited with saying, "Imagination is more important than information."

Did you know that Einstein went fishing for ideas?

He would reportedly spend long, quiet hours on his sailboat, at times pulling out his notebook to jot down ideas as they came to him. And it's no wonder since gazing at water, or virtually anything in nature, tends to foster ideal conditions for creative problem-solving.

Risk-taking and play are other aspects of creativity that we naturally excel at as human beings.

---

3. Kamrul Hasan, *How AI quietly undermines the joy and effort of learning: a call for rebalancing education in the digital age*, 2025.

Just recently, I was walking with my son near an ice rink. He started climbing up a snow-covered hill, exploring all the nooks and crannies. He was fascinated by how the mound connected with the adjacent tree and wall.

To him, the formation was nothing short of magical. He was taking risks, but because they were within reason, I let him play. Not surprisingly, I can attest that my son often comes up with amazing ideas I never would have thought of.

In contrast, AI tends to be risk-averse. Rarely will it take a stance, give a strong opinion, or explore ideas unless it is programmed to do so within very well-defined parameters. Even then, the output is fundamentally different from what a human would create during creative exploration.

Finally, a unique human component of creativity is emotional engagement, i.e., creation for its own sake rather than for its usefulness. Whenever we program a prompt into AI, we are telling it what to create. But when humans are in a creative mood, they can create without boundaries. Imagine drawing an abstract shape and finding that it forms a beautiful image of a ship. Then, turning the oars into ears, and making the ship a human face.

Countless great works of art were created as happy accidents or at least contain some element of imperfection or exploration that makes them truly unique and unforgettable. This, too, is part of creativity.

This being said, AI can augment these capacities. One way is by reframing problems. With the right prompt, we can have AI present us with the same problem from different perspectives.

This can be extremely useful and falls under my 3R framework (Research, Rounding out, and Refining), which we will cover later in this book.

It can also connect disparate ideas to form something new. In other words, it can synthesize information and spark new ways of looking at things.

## Cultivating critical thinking

One pillar of critical thinking is to consider multiple perspectives, but AI will not do this unless we specifically tell it to. Even then, it's easy to get stuck in cognitive bias. By contrast, humans (however imperfect) can synthesize more organically and weigh different viewpoints, according to multiple internal and external barometers. We also have a high tolerance for ambiguity. We can be comfortable without having clear answers. In fact, one of my business mentors, Danny Iny, often says that one trait of highly successful entrepreneurs is their ability to sit with ambiguity. In contrast, AI is typically given a prompt to solve a problem. It will tend to sound authoritative because it has been specifically programmed to sound fluent and confident.

A second pillar of critical thinking is questioning assumptions. When my son watches TV, I sometimes ask him later, "Hey, do you think that's always true?" Or "What do you think is better, this or that?" I'm trying to teach him to think critically about what he sees. This is an important part of being a responsible citizen: daring to question things and considering bias, prejudice, and implicit assumptions.

AI may identify some instances, but because it is a recombining mechanism drawing on mountains of data from all kinds of sources (including discussion forums like Reddit and social media), it frequently makes uncritical assumptions. It won't challenge whoever is running the prompt.

Here again, however, AI can supplement critical thinking.

Gathering and evaluating evidence from different sources is another aspect of critical thinking. For a human, this can be very painstaking. But AI can instantly gather information from a wide range of sources. This can be done using fact-checked AI engines like Perplexity that choose specific types of sources. This is another of the 3Rs (research) we will cover. Even so, whatever the machine comes up with, a human must exercise judgment and choose a course of action based on perception and balanced analysis.

## Keeping it real, keeping it human

There is a real danger of seeing our brains atrophy in the AI era if we delegate critical thinking, creativity, and judgment to machines. But if we learn to tap into our own human qualities first and Give it our Personal Touch (GPT) before turning to AI, then it is remarkable what we can achieve. And we can feel good about it.

A great example is in the lines you are reading. I dictated this book using an app that transcribes spoken words and corrects basic grammar, making the text ready for editing by a serious human. I enjoy this workflow. It fits my natural style as a speaker and instructor, and allows me to create on my terms.

Importantly, every word in this book is mine. The ideas are mine. But AI handled the time-consuming work of copying the words I spoke, putting them into paragraphs, and fixing basic writing issues.

The key takeaway is to start with your own heart, mind, and soul.

Hone your intuition, creativity, and imagination.

Then, when you use technology, including AI if you so choose, it can augment your production in ways previously unimaginable.

In chapter four, we're going to look at a few fascinating, effective, enjoyable workflows that illustrate this.

## Key Insights

❖ AI can help draft, but humans cover the "last mile." Judgment, accountability, and real-world decisions remain human.

❖ Tools assist with human direction. Professionals choose the workflow and are responsible for the outcome.

❖ Just say no to "AI slop." Real value doesn't come from underpaid clean-up work, but from pros who use AI to enhance speed and quality.

❖ Protect imagination. Curiosity, play, risk-taking, and emotions foster creativity in ways AI cannot.

❖ Don't outsource thinking. Let AI gather and reframe information, but question, weigh, and decide.

❖ Start with your heart, mind, and soul, then use AI. Lead with your ideas and voice, use critical thinking, then let AI refine and accelerate your work, not replace you.

# Chapter Four

# The Creative Connection

***"To create means to relate. The root meaning of the word art is 'to fit together,' and we do this every day."***

-Corita Kent, artist, educator, and social justice advocate

Whether we're looking to create something, generate an insight, or make a tough call, using AI impulsively and thoughtlessly often reflects an inner lack of trust in ourselves.

In turn, this lack of self-trust is the natural consequence of a world that keeps us distracted and chasing after short-term gratification.

And although we'd like to think that school has prepared us for the "real world," it was never designed to overcome the irresistible itch to check our social media, listen to a soundbite on YouTube, or ask an AI any question and see what wondrous magic it comes up with.

In this chapter, we're going to go over an actionable framework for prompting YouGPT before resorting to AI.

## Your journey matters

Artificial intelligence focuses on a destination or a deliverable, but creating is also about the journey and what we learn and develop along the way.

I worked with an international team that co-created a meaningful presentation, putting together a brand narrative, expressing a powerful position on why and how they do things, and establishing guidelines for people wanting to work with them.

Creating the presentation was transformational for them. Not only in terms of the positive impact it created across the company and on clients, but also in terms of their own self-respect, empowerment, and ownership.

In business, creation is a critical vehicle because of the strategic thinking and buy-in it requires to develop.

Creating something, whether alone or as part of a team, helps sharpen judgment, clarify a position, and set us apart. It also helps us make better decisions that demonstrate our Alignment and Integrity (AI). And really, what is business other than a series of decisions?

But there is so much more involved in the act of creating.

Whether it's creating a common vision for our business or team, setting up innovation loops, or crafting a mission, creation demands a space to connect with ourselves and others. That's why we must use our GPT—to give our business endeavors that personal touch before turning to AI.

What's more, when we create something, let's say it's a plan for a product launch, we're prototyping. That is, we're getting something out of our heads and onto paper.

This requires us to make distinctions, compare and contrast different factors and considerations, and use critical thinking.

A plan is an empty shell without humans. But when it's given our personal touch, it takes on a core of meaning.

By using what we learn in this chapter, you'll be able to go beyond transactional AI use and move toward empowered creation and better outcomes.

## You are a creator

On a personal level, creating something, even for business, shapes us as creators.

We start to see ourselves not only as workers or leaders, but as creators with the agency and power that come with the decisiveness required to create something and put it out into the world.

It strengthens our confidence, deepens our mastery, and builds our authority. After all, "author" is the root word in "authority"!

The act of creation also rewires our brain and cultivates our uniquely human abilities, activating networks of emotion, memory, imagination, and embodied problem-solving.[1]

It's a cognitive and emotional workout. Although it takes time and effort, there's no limit to the rewards and satisfaction it brings.

One of this book's goals is to help you turn on your creator switch.

So many experts and professionals are caught up in their daily to-do lists and are just getting by.

Whether you're an entrepreneur or intrapreneur (which any employee can become), the more you create, the more you step into your power. And better yet, the more you'll want to create.

Creating is also an act of connection.

It requires that you plug into yourself and literally connect different parts of your brain, which creates a basis for connecting with others and even the world.

1. Roger E. Beaty, Cerebrum, *The Creative Brain*, 2020.

## The joy of exploration

Something I have thoroughly enjoyed doing over the years is spending my work breaks filling in adult coloring books. I buy them on Etsy and use professional-grade markers with vibrant colors. Occasionally, when I send a thank-you card to a client, I will include one of my coloring projects.

My clients' response has been profound. They're surprised, even shocked, to receive a work of art as a thank-you note.

It didn't take me any longer to create it than it did to sit on my futon during my work break. But for the client, it's a deeply meaningful gift and an act of connection.

It's impossible to express how much I love creating these projects, how deeply rewarding it feels in my soul, and how joyful I am to give them to people who matter to me.

Another aspect of creation worth addressing is the distinction between the end and the means.

In his book *Le meilleur de soi* (the best of yourself), Guy Corneau tells the tale of a wealthy but deeply unhappy businessman whose therapist suggested he paint as part of his treatment.

He was reluctant because he didn't see himself as a creator or artist at all. But his therapist surprised him by clarifying that the goal wasn't to sell the paintings, but rather, to deliberately burn the paintings afterward.

There is a deeply transformative lesson here if we dig for the gold.

In Western societies, we are inculcated with the idea that whenever we do something, we do so to achieve a goal. We see our activities as a means to an end. We no longer do them for their own sake. We spend our entire lives chasing after goals, school grades, performance reviews, and work results.

This story illustrates that when we create, focusing too much on the result and tying it to our own personal worth gets in the way of the creative process. As a result, we often stop creating. We've become too perfectionistic, afraid the result won't meet a certain grade or standard.

So, when we create something for our business, it's important to adopt a mindset of not hanging on too tightly to what we create. The more tightly we grip our figurative brush, the choppier and more fragmented our creation will be.

A trained artist holds their brush lightly. And a master holds their creativity very lightly indeed!

The concept of destroying what we create is a wonderful way to let our minds know in advance that we're not creating to perform. We're creating for the sake of creating.

I recently had an interesting experience at a social gathering with my wife and a few friends. After some enjoyable conversation, we all loosened up and started playing the board game Pictionary. When it was my turn to draw on the canvas, I felt exuberant, something I've rarely experienced before or since.

I drew as I'd never drawn before. My wife was shocked. Later, in the car, she said, "We've been together for nearly 20 years. I didn't know you could draw!" I answered that I didn't either.

But in that moment, I was proud of my drawings because they were born of a good mood, of a state of relaxation, and of not caring about the outcome. I felt connected to myself and my friends at the party, which made the ideas and images flow effortlessly.

It can be difficult to find the Goldilocks zone where we can create from a space of joy and connection rather than misery and obligation.

So, let's look at a powerful way to start creating for business purposes: journaling.

## How journaling can work for you

I have journals in every room of my house. Some are clearly labeled, many are not. When I have an idea, I grab a journal and start writing. I'm not doing it to accomplish anything. But at some point in my life, I flipped on my creator switch.

Since then, I have had an irrepressible urge to create something every day. Most of what I create is in written form. I also have a more structured way of writing that helps me come up with my best insights and ideas, which I can augment with AI later if I so choose.

Here's the process if you'd like to give it a try. Find a quiet spot, get out a physical pen and journal, take a few deep breaths, jot down a question, and then write your name after it. You might ask, "What should I offer my clients next month?" Begin by writing your first name, and once the pen starts moving on the page, let it continue without censoring yourself.

During this process, try not to tell your thoughts what direction to take.

In my experience, it's a bit of a mystery where the answers come from. Some people believe it's channeling. Others, more scientific types, might say you've connected to your subconscious or linked different parts of your brain.

At the end of the day, we may never have a clear answer to that question, but the insights you will gain from this simple process are surprising and speak for themselves.

When I journal this way, it feels like the answers are reminding me of something I already knew deep down. In the journaling process, I'm able to put that thing into words, giving it structure and form. During these 15- to 20-minute journaling sessions, I feel expansive and clear. I can relax physically and mentally. And after, I feel like I can smile and go about my day feeling confident and inspired.

Once I finish writing the answer, I always end the session by noting my main insight, reframing, or action step.

I have brought this framework together in my **PRIDE** journaling method, which looks like this:

**P**ause and protect territory

**R**egulate with deep breaths

**I**nquire with a guiding question

**D**eclare presence (your name, and a comma)

**E**xtract a reframe or action at the end

That's how I came up with the ideas for this book. I developed the concepts over the course of many talks, conversations, readings, and reflections in different public and private forums. Then, one morning, I woke up knowing that I was ready to get my ideas down on paper. So, I followed the PRIDE method, got out some paper, went into a deep, focused relaxation, and let the ideas bubble up. The text was barely legible, but I was later able to dictate the ideas, then let AI organize them into chapters.

This brings me to how we can use AI alongside journaling.

Journaling apps are popular today, but personally, I use pen and paper. I've found that this is more effective for connecting different parts of the brain. There is some research to support this.[2] The act of putting pen to paper and creating in the 3D physical world, where we can see what we have written, often seems to deepen reflection.

During this process, it's essential not to censor yourself or judge your creations. Ask the question, then let the answer emerge and write it down.

---

2. Paolo Taurisano (Ed.), *The Neuroscience Behind Writing: Handwriting vs. Typing—Who Wins the Battle?*, 2025.

Hold this process lightly and capture the ideas before they disappear. Once they're gone, you may never get them back.

I guide individuals and teams through this process in my business consulting. The insights and reframes are nothing short of transformational.

## AI-augmented journaling

AI can be a very supportive aid for insight journaling. For example, you can devise journaling prompts by using AI to come up with questions to ask yourself. You might ask AI, "Hey, I have this problem. What are seven different questions I could ask myself to approach it from different angles?"

If there are thought leaders who inspire you, you can also tell AI, "Write seven journaling prompts on this topic inspired by so-and-so."

If no one comes to mind, try pulling up ChatGPT now and asking for seven business development journaling prompts inspired by Joachim Lépine. This can open myriad perspectives, without putting AI in control of your creative process.

Once we have reframes and insights from our journaling, we can turn to AI to help us flesh out a vision or provide action steps. The more specific the prompts, the more effective the process will be.

Whether you're writing your hero story, crafting a vision for your team, setting your yearly goals as a decision-maker, creating a compelling brand presentation, or drafting a pitch, try the PRIDE journaling method today. The magic here is not in the reading but in the doing.

In the next chapter, we'll be digging deep to define your custom "AI": Alignment and Integrity.

## Key Insights

❖ The creation journey matters. The process builds judgment, ownership, and alignment, not just the end result.

❖ Think of yourself as a creator. Creating cultivates confidence, fosters mastery, builds authority, and develops your uniquely human abilities.

❖ Loosen your grip on outcomes. When you create for the sake of creating, you escape perfectionism and unlock flow.

❖ Creation deepens connection. Even small, handmade creations you gift to others can be a powerful act of caring and meaning.

❖ Use PRIDE journaling to access YouGPT. Relax, ask, write freely, and then extract one core reframe or action.

❖ Allow AI to support your insights. Journal first to find your voice. Then use AI to refine, expand, and organize your ideas.

# Chapter Five

# Your AI: Alignment and Integrity

***"The biggest problem I see among people who want to excel in chess—and in business and in life in general—is not trusting their instincts enough."***

-Gary Kasparov

## Real intelligence: alignment and integrity

Beyond buzzwords and corporate speak, what values do we need to align with to build a thriving and rewarding business? And what does integrity mean in an AI-driven world?

In terms of alignment, being clear about your business values is a key part of career development, whether as an entrepreneur or an intrapreneur. As a solopreneur, clear values serve as a heuristic and decision filter, helping you make better, faster calls and build resonance and buy-in with clients and business partners.

As an employee, finding overlap between your values and your employer's is a fantastic way to foster a sense of belonging and motivation. It's a regular and valuable part of aligning personal and organizational values.

But how many values should we have?

Core values tend to range from three to seven or more in most organizations.[1]

However, to maximize focus and memorability, I recommend starting with only three values. More than three can lead to sprawl. Fewer than three will often fail to cover all the bases undergirding your business.

My core values are pride, courage, and integrity. All have played a critical role in my personal background and evolution.

Our personal background can be a wonderful source of inspiration in defining our values. The more clearly we articulate and showcase them, the more our content and offerings will resonate with like-minded people.

It took me many years to take pride in myself, as embodied by the lion symbol that appears in my marketing and on a large canvas in my office.

When I coach quiet experts and entrepreneurs, I find that many lack pride and self-belief. This hinders their progress and business growth. To be successful in business and life, conviction and self-confidence are essential.

1. Rhythm Systems, *Leveraging Core Values to Drive Revenue and Increase Profit*, 2024.

When I was younger, I was painfully shy. It took me a long time to trust myself and dare to embody who I really was deep down. I'm an introvert who's always been obsessed with self-improvement, business growth, and excellence on a personal and professional level. It took a lot of courage to step out of my comfort zone, learn to make offers, and speak to large audiences.

None of it came easy for me. That's why courage is my second value. I know that baby steps work, and I'm helping others with that today. And, finally, I'm a big believer in integrity. In other words, doing what we say we're going to do, being honest with ourselves and others, and staying true to our values even when it isn't popular.

This has helped me to pivot after making mistakes and attract the right partners to secure long-term success. How about you? If you had to choose three values you identify with at a soul level, what would they be?

Here's a table to help you pick a few. Take a moment for self-reflection. Start by selecting some values that resonate with you, then narrow down your list. Which three are closest to your heart and would you never operate without?

| **Integrity** | **Mastery** | **Connection** | **Impact** | **Performance** | **Freedom** |
|---|---|---|---|---|---|
| Integrity | Learning | Empathy | Service | Excellence | Freedom |
| Honesty | Curiosity | Compassion | Contribution | Results | Independence |
| Trust | Mastery | Caring | Impact | Performance | Flexibility |
| Fairness | Progress | Respect | Community | Discipline | Choice |
| Responsibility | Competence | Collaboration | Leadership | Precision | Adventure |
| Accountability | Growth | Connection | Legacy | Reliability | Innovation |
| Transparency | Wisdom | Kindness | Generosity | Consistency | Autonomy |

## Values meet vision

When I talk about alignment in this book, I mean aligning our values with our vision. The clearer our vision of success, the more successful we will tend to be.

Some time ago, I read a story about how Jim Carrey wrote himself a $10 million check, "for acting services rendered." He reportedly post-dated it for Thanksgiving 1995, put it in an envelope, and carried it in his wallet.

Six months before the due date, he was earning almost that much for *Dumb & Dumber*. His one-minute interview on this is surprising and very insightful.[2]

If Jim Carrey writing himself a check worked, I figured it could work for me, too. So, in the 2010s, I wrote down how much I wanted to earn each year. Of course, my amount wasn't as ambitious as his, but I wanted to continue practicing my profession as a translator and stay realistic!

A few years later, I accomplished that goal, and it felt like the most natural thing in the world.

Beyond writing myself a check, the main driver in accomplishing that goal was hiring a business coach to help me make better decisions, follow through on my action plans, and honestly admit what was working and what wasn't.

Writing down our goals is truly magical. We mustn't allow things to float around in our heads forever.

For me, writing is a sacred act. I think of words as portals to new versions of ourselves and our lives.

---

2. Renée Onque, CNBC, *Jim Carrey wrote himself a $10 million check before he could cash it—a few years later, he did: Here's the science behind manifestation*, 2026.

Here are some prompts to help you reflect on your own goals:

*Where do you want to be in one year?*

*If we were making a toast one year from now, what would we be celebrating?*

*Where would you be?*

*What would you be doing?*

*Who would you be doing it with?*

*How much would you be making?*

*How would you be helping people?*

Be specific. Describe and quantify as much as possible.

This is a space for human-first exploration, not perfection, or an immutable, one-and-done vision.

My vision has changed quite a bit over the years. In the 2000s, I would have been content with a fully booked translation business. But by the end of the 2010s, my vision had evolved to 50% training and coaching. Today, my vision is to speak on major stages, share my message of human-first workflows in the AI era, and provide world-class courses, coaching, and consulting to businesses and organizations of all sizes. I want to help more people, more profoundly, with what I've learned.

Whatever your individual or company vision, I challenge you to write it down.

A coaching client recently told me, "I don't want to write down my goals because I'm afraid I won't achieve them." This is a crucial sticking point. Consider this reframe: We don't write down goals to achieve exactly those things on specific dates. That's not the point. Life happens, and we may or may not achieve our exact goal. The point is that there is inherent value in imagining, just as there is in creating.

Sitting down and daring to write exactly where we want to be primes us for success and helps us take ownership of our goals. It's also an act of connection with ourselves and our subconscious or higher power, depending on our beliefs.

There are two ways to view my success after writing down and achieving my income goal: One is more woo-woo and the other more pragmatic.

First, this was manifestation. I focused on my goal with positive emotion. Therefore, I attracted it. This is the thought process epitomized by Rhonda Byrne's best-selling book *The Secret*.

The other is more pragmatic. When we write down our goals, we engage our reticular activating system and start noticing opportunities we would have missed before. We also begin to make decisions that align with our new self-image. Then, before we know it, we're making progress. Daily micro-decisions add up to thousands of shifts, and in a year or two, achieving a lofty goal is not unheard of.

At the end of the day, it doesn't matter which view you subscribe to. What matters is that it works.

Once you've written down your goal, consider displaying it in your office (or in your wallet!). This is important. Remember, you are building your own AI (Alignment and Integrity) to lay the foundation for your business success.

## From Vision to Mission

What is your broader mission in your professional life?

Today, my mission is to help experts and entrepreneurs build thriving businesses through human-first strategy and workflows.

What's yours?

A simple way to narrow down your mission is to say, "I help XYZ person or organization achieve ABC outcome."

If you're employed, you might ask, "Do I really need a mission?" I would answer, yes. When we have a sense of purpose about what we do, it completely changes the way we approach our work.

In a popular video, leadership expert Robin Sharma interviewed a joyful airport bathroom attendant he met on a visit to South Africa. Robin asked the attendant what he was so happy about. The attendant told him that he didn't see himself as a bathroom attendant; he loved his work and took pride in it because he found meaning in his mission. He saw himself as people's first point of contact with Africa, and he wanted to make sure that their first experience in his country was positive and unforgettable.

This is the difference between going through the motions and having a mission, regardless of professional title. It's all about the meaning we assign to our work.

What's your mission? Take some time to reflect on who you help and why it matters to you so deeply.

*What do you love about your work?*

*What gives your work meaning, beyond the immediate actions you perform?*

*Why are you proud to do what you do?*

## But what if you're multi-passionate?

Not everyone will have just one mission, especially if you do more than one thing in your work life.

If you're multi-passionate, it can be challenging to pin down a once-and-for-all mission or overly constraining purpose for who you are. Instead, it can help to think in terms of a general direction.

Let's say you're a teacher like me. You will always be teaching in some form, and it will always be deeply rewarding.

Being clear on that is a huge step forward. It's freeing in that as long as you're teaching in any form, whether you're standing in front of a classroom or writing a how-to book, you know that you're fulfilling your purpose. You don't have to second-guess every potential career choice anymore or overanalyze it to death. What a relief!

Maybe you're not a born teacher, but a data analyst at heart. With a razor-sharp analytical mind, you instantly draw connections between things and piece together complex data to form a coherent narrative that helps people in some way. My financial advisor fits this profile. You are also contributing your unique qualities to make a better world. Don't be shy about owning your mission, or even just a general direction.

We're going to look at how we can augment the clearly defined vision, values, and mission we already have with AI. But first, a caveat.

### The big AI lie, or how not to use AI to grow your business

The "one-click myth" is everywhere today, but it's just that, a myth. Except for a few outliers, the people using AI effectively to grow their business are doing so strategically. What's more, implementation, analysis, and reiteration are often more important than the output you get from a chatbot.

This is reassuring in a way. The game hasn't changed as much as some app developers would have us believe.

Today, successful businesspeople tend to have clear values. They have a vision and a mission, and they make better decisions as a result. Strategy, analysis, and recalibration still beat throwing spaghetti at the wall.

So, while everyone is asking AI bots to give them miracle cures, I'm going to suggest something different from the instant wins adorning our Facebook and Insta feeds (which, ironically, are often produced by AI instead of humans).

We should use generative AI to amplify our capabilities and assets.

## When to turn to AI

It can be helpful to have a simple framework for deciding when to use AI, when to rely only on humans because of the human qualities that add value, and when to use them together.

To help us make this decision, I've devised a simple matrix. It's called the **FAR** matrix. It stands for:

**F**it for automation

**A**dded value of using AI

**R**isk

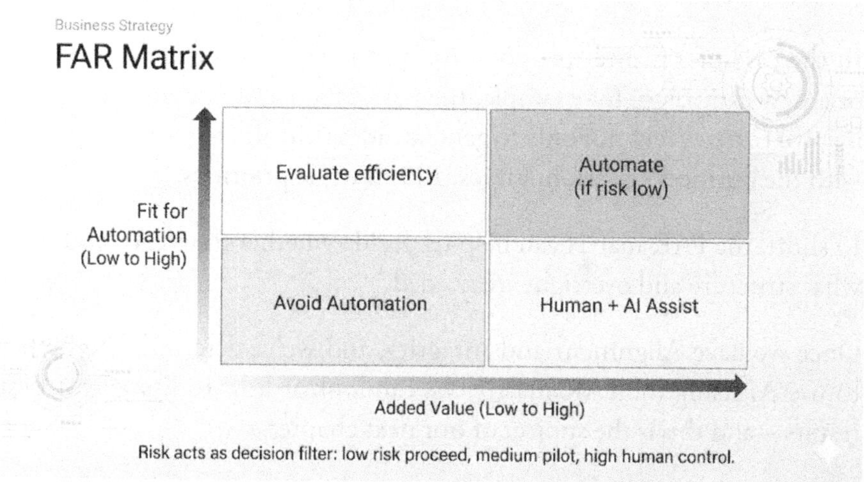


Mastering this matrix can help us bring our best selves to every task and determine what to hand off to machines.

Here's a simple way to remember the matrix: "How FAR do I want to go using AI for this task?"

The first question is: **"Is the task Fit for automation?"** In other words, does it involve heavily patterned information, predictable procedures, and a heavy information load? If so, AI can usually assist.

An example would be AI-generating a report to extract insights that will help inform pillars for content marketing.

The second question is: **"Does AI really Add value compared to humans or even a non-AI technology?"** Is it worthwhile when considering the environmental impact and other costs? What is the trade-off and is it worthwhile?

Finally, the R in the FAR matrix stands for risk: **"What is the Risk of using AI?"** Could a serious mistake be costly in this case? Equally importantly, do we have review and oversight in place? This is a good time to factor in confidentiality risks, which we will examine further on. AI can be hacked, especially when assets aren't properly secured.

In the case of a project proposal for a top client or the announcement of a new campaign, for example, the risk is high and humans need to be involved extensively, not only to generate ideas but also to ensure they align with the business's mission, values, and strategic priorities.

In short, the FAR matrix can help us decide whether to use AI, and if so, what structure and oversight are needed.

Once we have Alignment and Integrity, and we've determined whether to use AI using the FAR matrix, we can look at how to use AI for best results—and this is the subject of our next chapter.

## Key Insights

❖ Alignment equals lived values. In an AI world, true alignment means acting from clear values, not buzzwords.

❖ Have three values for maximum focus. Limiting yourself to three core values lets you make decisions faster and clearer.

❖ If you're struggling to define your values, look to your past and what has made you the unique person you are today.

❖ Choosing three soul-level values aligns your vision, work, and life.

❖ Use the FAR Matrix to decide whether to use AI. Check whether a task is Fit for automation, whether AI would genuinely Add value, and whether it's worthwhile given the Risks involved.

# Chapter Six

# Look Within, Find Without

***"Give us the tools, and we will finish the job."***

-Winston Churchill

Once you've resolved to use generative AI for augmentation, a good way to remember the ideal order of operations is my **STAR** framework:

**S**tart with the end in mind

**T**une in to yourself

**A**ugment the result using the 3Rs (Research, Round out, Refine)

**R**eiterate

Here's a simple example: Last week, I was asked to give a presentation on sales skills for professionals and experts in the AI era.

So, I began with the end in mind (the S in STAR)—crafting a five-star, two-hour presentation with lots of great sales advice and anecdotes to delight my audience.

Next, I tuned into myself by taking a walk and speaking all my ideas into my phone (the T in STAR).

I subsequently had my app put my spoken text into written form, correct grammatical errors, and organize the content into buckets to form speakers' notes (the A in STAR).

Finally, I turned to ChatGPT and used follow-up prompts to reiterate until the content was neither too short, nor too long—just the right length (the R in STAR).

The result was phenomenal. And I was even able to repurpose my speakers' notes into a dazzling slide deck using a separate AI-powered app!

In short, the STAR sequence helps reduce the delta between original intent and final creation, so that the final result feels natural, aligned, and compelling.

Let's now look at some of the main AI tools on the market, and how you can use them in conjunction with the STAR framework to achieve phenomenal results.

## Which AI to use?

ChatGPT is best known for its versatility and brainstorming; Gemini for its search capabilities and Google Suite integration; Claude for its long-form content and complex instructions; and Perplexity for fact-checking. Microsoft is good for productivity and Microsoft integration; Grok for speed and conversational prowess; Mistral for European language integration; and Llama (from Meta) for its community ecosystem.

To begin, try the following prompts with Claude or ChatGPT for more creative tasks, and with Perplexity for accuracy and real-time research insights.

## Values

Writing down your core values is a great first step. Because it excels at pattern recognition and has been trained on a vast trove of business data, AI can help us determine how to act in alignment with these values and identify red flags to watch for. Try this prompt:

*You are a world-class business-growth consultant helping me embed values into my operations. For each core value [write your values here], provide five specific behaviors that can be observed, coached, and evaluated. Then outline three counterproductive behaviors that clearly undermine each value.*

This will provide you with a handy checklist of down-to-earth dos and don'ts to help you reach your next level as an entrepreneur or intrapreneur.

## Vision

AI can also help us think about how to bring a vision to life. The key is giving the bot a very clear vision. Here's the prompt:

*You are a world-class strategist for business growth and execution. Translate my existing business vision [describe here] into a 12-month strategic roadmap that includes market positioning, differentiation, the revenue model, and key milestones. Convert this into quarterly OKRs with clear objectives, measurable key results, and prioritized actions that align the team and drive scalable execution.*

When I've run this prompt, I've found the 12-month plan is a little too ambitious to put into practice, but several OKRs (objectives and key results) have been extremely helpful to consider as success indicators to track over the coming year.

## Mission

Mission is very personal, but AI can help here too. Once we have a solid draft, try this prompt for further clarity and refinement:

*You are a critical business strategist. My mission is (enter mission), and I help ABC clients achieve XYZ outcome. Identify five overused, vague mission clichés common in this space that should be avoided. Then craft three bold, differentiated mission statements without using any of those clichés. Each mission must be under 15 words and articulate a clear, tangible customer outcome.*

## Further resources

Once our Alignment and Integrity are defined, in the form of our values, vision, and mission, we can use AI to find powerful resources that help us succeed in almost any endeavor we can imagine.

It's easy to feel overwhelmed by the new AI apps coming out every day. The solution is to shift away from the endless cycle of buying, testing and abandoning AI apps, and toward "just-in-time" purchases.

The key is to take a few moments to write down what you want to achieve. Only then should you use AI to find the right tools for the job.

Let's face it, the tools will continue to evolve. On the day this book is released, new apps will be available on the market.

The important thing is, remember to always tap into YouGPT first.

When you're clear on your direction, AI can be very useful at finding the right tools to help you succeed. For example, go to Perplexity and say:

*I plan to [describe goal] within one year. Suggest 37 AI-driven apps and resources that can help me do so and prioritize the apps involving human-first workflows that align with my values.*

The number 37 is arbitrary, but helps provide a sufficient range to surface interesting apps.

When I did this, I saw several apps I was already using, but I also found one or two that I hadn't explored. This is a great way to ensure our AI use is well-aligned and just-in-time.

Here is a new mantra, particularly for AI-obsessed technophiles:

*Forget "just in case." Buy business resources "just in time."*

## "Quick-hits" business help

Many coaches today sell custom bots for coaching or specific tasks, such as crafting social media content.

I used GrahamAI for a few months. It's a custom AI chatbot coach trained on business mentor Graham Cochrane's courses and YouTube videos, which I follow. Once I came up with ideas for social media posts or newsletters, I'd ask GrahamAI for critical feedback.

Some of its insights were gold. Others didn't feel right or didn't align with my vibe.

Even though I have a great real-life business coach and turn to several consultants and advisors for different things, GrahamAI helped me get unstuck in the short term and make several better business decisions. The small monthly investment was worth it.

## Situational breakthroughs

Another way to get immediate assistance from AI is to ask a specific source for help.

For example, I made a joke at a social gathering that landed totally flat. Then, moments later, I watched someone else in the group make the very same joke, to raucous laughter and applause.

So, I went to ChatGPT and wrote:

*Based on the insights of Charisma on Command (whose YouTube channel I love and recommend), tell me why my jokes aren't landing, even though they obviously work when other people tell them. What's wrong with my delivery?*

It gave me an extraordinarily useful insight—namely, that people who tell successful jokes in social settings:

1) Speak a little louder than they normally would.

2) Are confident that people will laugh after the joke.

3) Often use some exaggerated body language to make it clear that what they said was intended to be funny.

This is the opposite of "testing," where you timidly tell a joke hoping someone will laugh.

I realized my mistake instantly. I was testing my jokes. Because I was with a rowdy group of people talking at once, to cut through the noise, I had to speak a little louder, and project a level of self-assurance I *expected* would make people laugh at the joke.

I tried doing this in my next conversation and was finally rewarded with laughter.

AI can provide insights from specific sources, helping us get unstuck or get immediate assistance in a variety of contexts.

We can think of everyday situations when we get stuck. A bot might provide a situational insight, without requiring a huge investment of time or money.

AI can also be used for time-intensive tasks, such as validating market demand or running marketing campaigns.

## Business growth as a creative pursuit

Like chess grandmaster Gary Kasparov, I like to think of business as a game.

As a teenager, I was active in my school's chess club. I played against masters and competed in tournaments.

But my favorite part of chess was the craft of strategy. I loved sitting down with strategy books, going over famous grandmaster games on a chessboard in my room.

Often, one of my brothers would pop in and say sarcastically, "Hey, Joe, who's winning?" and I would get flustered and angry.

But in retrospect, those years of chess lessons and games were invaluable. Because I'm a more creative, right-brain-dominant type, those years helped me merge my love of strategy, which came naturally to me, with hard tactics and foresight, predominantly left-brain activities.

Today, I approach business a lot like playing chess. It's always about the next move and the next decision.

What works best is not to give up our personality, but to lean into it more, just like the chess grandmasters who have a particular style they're known for.

When we're clear about our values, and we consult YouGPT first, AI becomes an amplifier.

Here's a Kasparov-inspired prompt:

*Based on Gary Kasparov's insight that success mainly depends on knowing how to handle failure, design a bold 3-month growth-strategy sprint that assumes intelligent risk, builds rapid feedback loops from mistakes, and converts every setback into compounding strategic advantage over competitors. Make it specific to me and my situation [enter details].*

## Emotional processing

A few weeks ago, I posted on LinkedIn about creating a guidebook to help people get more views. Afterward, someone left a critical comment. They implied that I was promoting hustle-bro culture. This couldn't be farther from the truth. The goal of the post was to help others get more client bookings ethically by producing content that would connect more deeply with their audience. But the damage was done, and I felt upset after reading that comment.

So, I went to YouGPT after taking a few deep breaths. I thought, "Why does this upset me?" And I did a bit of journaling.

But I still felt off my game. So, I went to ChatGPT again, this time in a private, temporary chat, and explained the nature of my post and the comment. Rather than just allowing ChatGPT to answer, I prompted it to break down why the comment upset me so I could process it better. The prompt went something like this:

*This incident happened on LinkedIn: [describe here]. Ask me one question at a time to help unpack why it upset me. When I'm done venting, give me your analysis and feedback.*

This conversation helped peel back the layers of emotion surrounding the incident.

For example, I realized that deep down, I was afraid of coming across as salesy or hustle-bro-ish on social media, because that would be inconsistent with my values. The reader had interpreted my post that way, but crucially, it didn't mean my post was inappropriate. I realized I was in my lane and I hadn't said anything wrong or out of step.

It helped me completely release any lingering negativity. I had maintained my integrity after all, so I didn't need to be ashamed of anything.

I would never dream of replacing my therapist with AI. When it comes to deep, long-term introspection and growth, I believe in turning to humans.

But for one-off assistance with analyzing and even de-escalating emotional situations, AI can be useful and play a complementary role when given the right prompts.

## AI interview prep

I was recently interviewed about the importance of putting people first in the knowledge professions today and about how to conceptualize our use of AI. The problem was that I hadn't had time to prepare for the interview questions.

On the bus ride to the studio, I jotted down all the key messages I wanted to convey from the heart and deliver in the videos.

It would've taken a long time to comb through all those key messages, anecdotes, and examples, categorize them, then reverse engineer an interview question for each category. In this case, I was able to turn to AI.

Once I had a draft of my clear messages, I asked AI to categorize them and craft insightful, inspiring interview questions to draw out the best of what I had to say in each category:

*Take these notes and organize them into seven one-page cheat sheets, each containing 3 brief questions I will answer during a live interview. Each sheet should focus on one key message.*

Then, I jotted down the questions in a journal. That way, I could glance at them from time to time during the interview.

Epilogue: Despite my nervousness, the interview went off without a hitch. You can view the video on my speaker website, joachimlepine.com.[1]

Now, let's turn to research and preparation, learning and insights, decision-making, social media, emails and other content, and more.

---

1. Joachim Lépine, *AI Changes Everything Except the Power of Trust*, 2026.

## Market research and optimization

When we want to check market demand for our product or service, we can use Perplexity. It's a fact-checked AI app that can analyze social media (with some restrictions). Here's a helpful prompt:

*You are a market research strategist who is vetting the launch of [insert product/service] for [target audience]. Summarize opportunities in the next 12 months with estimated market size and growth, key competitors with weaknesses, audience segments and pain points, ranked risks, and 3 overlooked growth angles with data-backed insights.*

New market research and optimization apps are coming out all the time. For example, if you have a YouTube channel, you can turn to Vidtechy and other apps for help with keywords and channel optimization. These kinds of tools will only become more prevalent in the coming years.

Finally, you can use your preferred AI app as a strategic sounding board. For example:

*Act like [a business expert you find insightful, such as Jeanna Gabellini]. I'm going to tell you about an offer I'd like to launch. We will have a back-and-forth conversation. Ask me insightful questions, one at a time, to draw out the information you need. Then give me your critical feedback on whether you think this is a good idea and how I can improve it.*

This is a wonderful, free way to get super helpful insights when you have ideas you want to refine.

## Learning and insights

Data synthesis is one of AI's superpowers. Besides the chatbots we're all familiar with, you can use Google's NotebookLM. It lets users upload up to 50 sources (PDFs, podcasts, YouTube videos, and more) in a notebook. As of this writing, you can have up to 100 notebooks free of charge.

Once the notebook is created, you can extract insights and chat back and forth with that curated dataset. The AI will also create information digests you can watch or listen to in order to help find and assimilate information.

Try this prompt in NotebookLM:

*Map out all the interconnected ideas around [core concept]. What other topics, assumptions, or implications does it silently touch upon, challenge, or depend on?*

## Learning "power up" prompts

In no specific order, here are some of the all-time highest-performing prompts I've used for my own business, concerning learning and insights in particular:

*Break down the topic of [ABC] for someone who is driven but busy. No fluff or theory, only actionable advice. Make it as simple as possible without watering down its essence.*

*Quiz me on topic [ABC] and identify what I don't know.*

*Summarize the five best-selling books on the topic of [ABC] into seven actionable steps.*

*Turn this [long tutorial, for example] into a simple checklist I can print and keep on my desk.*

*Tell me five things about the topic of [ABC] that insiders and professionals know but rarely share.*

*Simulate a round-table discussion between the top 3 experts in the field of [ABC] and me. Present their respective viewpoints and any areas in which we agree or disagree.*

Beyond prompts, AI is increasingly integrated into many learning platforms. For instance, the learning platform Udemy now has an AI assistant. You can ask, "What did the instructor say again about [subject ABC]?"

The assistant will find that information instantly and give it to you in an easy-to-assimilate form.

## Social media

AI can augment your social media posts and content.

One way to ensure you're thinking critically before having AI create your content is to use this prompt:

*Share three ways to achieve my Facebook/LinkedIn/Instagram goal of [ABC]. Include the pros and cons of each. Also, tell me when each approach works best.*

Another great prompt is to ask AI to analyze your post performance on your preferred social network, such as LinkedIn, considering your goals, and to provide critical pointers for improvement. The prompt might read like this:

*Analyze my posts on [preferred social media] and let me know how to optimize future posts to help me achieve my goal [for example, to double my follower count in 12 months].*

You can also have AI identify social trends in your niche. Many apps do this. Then, come up with post ideas that are likely to resonate with the right people. The more specific you are, the better the results you will get.

Make sure to tell AI you want it to be your social media strategist. Give it some preliminary ideas. Provide examples of social content you like and feel align with your values, and ask for different options to choose from.

You can also use AI to repurpose all manner of social media content.

You can use AI to surface psychological factors that can help you sell your services more effectively.

Here again, integrity and ethics are important.

Here's a prompt to try:

*Identify the beliefs someone would need before buying my product or service and devise a series of seven emails to help them develop those beliefs ethically, grounded in proof rather than hype.*

I wouldn't have AI write my emails, but sometimes I've used AI-recommended sequences that are helpful and true to my values.

## AI for writing emails

In Gmail's pro version, Gemini will suggest draft emails. But my favorite go-to is to write an email myself, then to put my draft into an AI and say:

*Give me 3 different ways I can say [ABC], from most neutral to most creative.*

This way, you can use AI to round out your emails, rather than have it write them for you.

## High-level decision-making

AI can be extraordinarily useful for high-level decision-making. Take some time to reflect on an ambitious goal you want to achieve. But know that when you turn to AI, you will need to provide good instructions for the bot to do its job well.

For example, you can sprinkle a few of the following parameters into your conversation:

*Think with me, not for me.*

*Hold the following context.*

*Never sacrifice rigor for reassurance.*

*Ask me one question at a time, asking me to confirm or correct your hypothesis before moving on.*

If you use the prompts and resources in this chapter, you will be light years ahead of the vast majority of business owners today.

This chapter has covered a variety of human-first workflows that can transform your research, preparation, learning, implementation, social media, emails, and decision-making.

Next, we're going to take a deep dive into mental models for the AI era.

## Key Insights

❖ A handy framework for getting the most out of AI augmentation is STAR: Start with the end in mind, Tune into yourself, Augment with AI, and Reiterate.

❖ AI amplifies alignment. When your values, vision, and mission are clear, AI becomes a force multiplier rather than a distraction.

❖ Prompts turn values into behavior. Thoughtful prompts translate abstract values into concrete, coachable actions and red flags.

❖ Use the right AI for the right job. Different tools excel at creativity, research, or execution. Strategy is choosing which ones to use and when.

❖ Shift from "just in case" to "just in time." You don't need every new, shiny app that comes along; you need the right AI support for the next step.

❖ AI unlocks situational breakthroughs. With thoughtful prompts, AI can provide real-time insights into your jokes, emotions, offers, and decisions.

❖ Business is a game of creation. When you consult YouGPT first, AI becomes your strategy partner rather than your replacement.

# Chapter Seven

# Your Inner OS: Mental Models for Human-First Thinking

***"The main thing is to keep the main thing the main thing."***

-Stephen R. Covey

So far, we've talked about the importance of putting people first, laid a foundation for business success, and gone over clever ways to start using AI to boost our efforts. Now, let's explore a few mental models that can help us make better, more strategic decisions about AI and many other things.

## First-principles thinking

When we're faced with complex decisions, especially involving innovation, it's easy to get stuck in analysis paralysis. This is especially true in business. There are many variables at play, and tweaking any of them will have a ripple effect on our entire business.

First-principles thinking can help by drilling down to the basics and re-building everything from scratch.

When we build from an irreducible truth, such as a core value rather than a tool or tactic, the results tend to be better. It's well documented that the most successful companies tend to start with a human problem and narrative before designing the solution, i.e., a specific tool or feature.[1] This helps prevent using technology for technology's sake and keeps values anchored in people and their needs.

As we've seen, a few irreducible building blocks worth establishing are our values (our beliefs), our vision (what success looks like), and our mission (why we do what we do). In business decision-making, these serve as practical first principles that guide decisions downstream. Solid first principles enable faster and better decisions.

Tactics must be an outgrowth of first principles. They are a subsequent layer and must be paired with feedback loops to make sure they align and work.

So many business problems can be traced back to a lack of clear values, vision, and mission. In particular, for founders and entrepreneurs, a lack of first principles can lead to "shiny object syndrome." In other words, constantly chasing after the latest trending tactic, for example, dangled in a Facebook ad, rather than building out aligned marketing assets and then tracking their performance and iterating incrementally over time.

The reason many tactics don't work isn't that they are inherently bad or ineffective. Rather, it's often because they don't align with first principles.

Here's an anecdote that illustrates first-principles thinking perfectly. At the end of each cohort of my flagship online course Squeak to Roar, I send each participant a phone holder engraved with their name, inscribed with the words "Badass CEO."

Although I share many bonuses and goodies with the people who take my high-ticket courses, so far, this phone holder has been the most popular. I've received countless emails about it.

---

1. Julia Binder and Michael D. Watkins, *To Solve a Tough Problem, Reframe It*, 2024.

Many of my students have proudly posted photos on social media of themselves holding their phone holders. And, as it turns out, this is great marketing for them and yours truly, their coach.

Sending people a phone holder might seem like a nice afterthought, but there's more to it than that. It's effective because it is underpinned by first-principles thinking.

In this case, I didn't ask myself, "What gift should I give people who take my flagship course?" (tactics-first thinking). Instead, I asked, "What am I trying to achieve for the people on the other side who take this course?" That is the irreducible building block.

Here, it's cementing the graduates' pride in their new identity as a Badass CEO. They feel great, remember to apply what they've learned, and become ambassadors for our brand.

People who receive this phone holder feel personally connected to their new identity as a Badass CEO.

That's the power of getting clear about what's truly important and only building out tactics in a second stage.

## How to apply first principles

The starting point of first-principles thinking is breaking down complex issues into their most foundational components, in other words, first principles.

Then using them as a launchpad for reasoning, rather than relying on assumptions, analogies, conventional wisdom, or even implicit biases we've picked up without realizing it.

First-principles thinking is often attributed to ancient Greek philosopher Aristotle, who believed in the importance of asking basic, sometimes even "stupid" or obvious questions until we arrive at an irreducible truth.

For me, knowing that pride, courage, and integrity are my core values helps me filter my decisions. Everything I do must align with these values. I strive to make my marketing assets an embodiment of my values, and people who resonate with them often reach out to me for a consultation or training call to assist their team.

Conversely, tactics not rooted in first principles, in the non-negotiables that matter most, generally don't work, or end up being a flash in the pan.

## Opportunity cost

Everything we do in life and business has an opportunity cost: We are choosing to do one thing rather than something else we could be doing. When we're too hasty in decision-making, we don't see the invisible opportunity cost. Any business owner who has agreed to work with a thankless, nitpicking client for a short-term payoff knows exactly what I'm talking about.

I help businesspeople dare to say no to misaligned opportunities, and then, to use the freed-up time to establish and align a strong brand, vision, mission, strategic priorities, and tactics, to attract the right clients. Now we're talking!

Even for businesspeople engaging in more outbound (prospecting) than inbound (client attraction) marketing, potential clients will always want to see who they are. Their brand's new alignment will also help convert outbound leads. So, whether we're more focused on attracting clients or pursuing them more aggressively, defining our brand is essential to our success.

Opportunity cost also applies to other contexts. If we choose to do low-value, redundant, administrative work manually when it could be outsourced to someone else or, in some cases, to a specialized AI, we take time and energy away from business planning, relationship building, creativity, development, and leadership training that could significantly boost our careers and businesses.

So, there is an argument to be made for delegating lower-value tasks as we migrate to higher-value tasks, whether we're stepping into our role as a high-value entrepreneur fully or moving up in our organization as an intrapreneur.

If a manager asks ChatGPT to write their onboarding procedure while providing a minimum of details, they may get something that looks nice at first glance. This is the "wow effect" AI often produces when its output is impressively humanlike.

But here, there's an opportunity cost.

If the manager uses AI unthinkingly, they surrender the opportunity to develop and clarify what does and doesn't really matter in their business, which can save them considerable time and headaches down the road.

Generic AI might sound impressive, but it's unlikely to be tailored to your circumstances or the daily tasks you need an employee to handle.

It's much more effective to sit down and brainstorm onboarding procedures that align with your vision, values, and strategic priorities. Then you can turn to AI to identify blind spots, such as tasks or steps that may have been overlooked. AI also excels at repurposing. It can take a list and convert it into a tidy, official-looking standard operating procedure.

In the long term, organizational data can be connected to a company-wide AI that can surface patterns, provide useful insights, and suggest optimized procedures. But the key in all cases is to start with genuine reflection and produce quality materials that serve as a basis for future efforts. Garbage in, garbage out.

## The inversion principle

Imagine two blog posts. In the first, the author uses AI like a vending machine, asking it to generate an article on what to include in a will.

They produce some generic content that sounds good at first but doesn't stand out or offer any fresh insights. It's like all the other AI-generated blogs out there on the same topic.

In the second blog, the author takes time to jot down the most frequently asked questions from clients about wills and testaments. They end up with a list of five common questions. Those are narrowed down to the number one most common, critical, and overlooked question on the topic. It could be, "Do you need a will in XYZ situation?" or "Can't AI just write it for you?"

While the first blog post collects dust, the human-written blog gets thousands of views, turning three readers into leads who book discovery calls to learn more.

The inversion principle applies here. Rather than asking, "How can I succeed?" the question becomes, "What would guarantee failure?"

With that knowledge, we avoid those moves.

In this case, AI may save time but also result in plain-vanilla content, critical errors stemming from AI hallucinations, and robotic content that even causes existing clients to disengage and ignore emails and newsletters.

Now we can see the value of the inversion principle. When we ask what would lead to failure and then avoid it, we can make better decisions more easily, especially when we feel overwhelmed by possibilities and are struggling to decide on the right path forward.

When I was younger, I couldn't decide on a career. I went to career counselors, asked everyone I knew for their opinion, completed a master's degree in education, all the while trying to figure it out, and still didn't feel any closer to deciding what I wanted to do in life.

Then, a wise man asked me, "What do you never want to do again?" I did not want to teach high school again. I admired high school teachers, but I didn't have the right disposition to work with students that age. This helped me decide to leave my job.

Walking away from my budding career as a high school music teacher was one of the hardest things I've ever had to do. But shortly after, I started seeing new opportunities everywhere in more aligned fields. I ended up going back to school to study translation and later became a teacher again, on my own terms, teaching university courses and professional development. I found my calling in adult education.

Finally, speaking of inversion, did you know that many companies conduct not only post-mortems but also pre-mortems? This practice is documented in decision-science research, as a way to combat overconfidence.[2] A pre-mortem helps anticipate obstacles and issues, ultimately leading to better choices.

Here, there's an interesting parallel with visualization. I read an interview with Olympian Michael Phelps in which he said he visualized not only winning but also responding to any number of problems that might come up during his next swimming race. Building a library of every possible scenario helped him break world records.[3]

This can also be tied to inversion. When we know what will fail and clearly define what we do not want, then, and only then, can we chart a successful path forward.

This also applies to choosing the right technologies, or none at all, for the job at hand.

## Systems thinking

Workflows do not exist in isolation, but are enmeshed with colleagues' and clients' morale, ethics, quality, and trust. Systems thinking is about considering the entire system rather than just one aspect.

---

2. Beth Veinott et al., *Evaluating the Effectiveness of the PreMortem Technique on Plan Confidence*, 2010.

3. J.D. Meier, *Sources of Insight, How Michael Phelps Used Visualization to Break World Records*, 2026.

I've spoken to several high-level AI strategists, and I've noticed a commonality. They all take the long view and think in systems. They're not just using AI to save time. In fact, if we use tools that save us ever-increasing time, we may end up becoming busier and more fragmented. Soon, we will find ourselves rushing aimlessly, going nowhere.

Imagine a small retailer using AI to forecast inventory. At first, it seems very impressive, but the machine imposes rigid auto-rules that lead to lower staff morale and burnout after a few months.

The problem is that AI optimized one thing, stock levels, but by the same token, it created unpredictable rush work for the people in receiving and logistics, so it was harmful to a different part of the system.

This is a real risk with AI integration. If not thought through, it can turn into doing whatever seems to save time. After all, time equals money for an employer. But when we change one aspect of a system, we inevitably affect all the others.

Instead, people who use AI strategically tend to perform the same tasks in the same amount of time but do them better thanks to the 3Rs (Research, Round out, Refine).

Now we can finally resolve the equation and make sense of AI integration. Strategic use of AI means clients get added value and we stay true to our core values.

## Secondary order effects

All changes have knock-on effects beyond the immediate situation. So, before implementing AI, it's worthwhile to ask how it might affect the company's culture, learning, skill development, client experience, and more. In business, time and money are readily measurable, but other fundamental, harder-to-quantify elements can fall by the wayside, leading to bottlenecks, delays, problems, burnout, and ultimately failure.

Take the example of a SaaS company that starts using an AI support chatbot to reduce support tickets.

At first, they're thrilled with the results because they receive fewer enquiries and assume the bot is providing everyone with what they need. However, they begin to notice an increase in churn. When they conduct interviews, which is always a smart move, they find their users feel unheard and disconnected.

The problem is that the founders optimized for low ticket volume rather than high customer trust and engagement. The second-order, or knock-on, effect wasn't speed, as anticipated, but erosion of the relationship signal that is so fundamental to a SaaS business. For SaaS founders, client satisfaction is their lifeblood.

## Chesterton's fence

Have you ever heard of Chesterton's Fence mental model? It can be summed up as, "Don't remove a process until you understand why it was created in the first place." The reason is that so-called inefficient processes often carry hidden value in the form of reflection, mentoring, development, craftsmanship, or trust-building.

Imagine a big company removes what it considers slow QA in the AI drafting stage for its next product launch. They get very few clicks and wonder what happened to the successful promotional efforts they've had in the past. After checking the metrics, they determine the content isn't landing with or converting readers.

It turns out the QA process wasn't only about detecting typos. It helped establish shared context and meaning, serving as an ethics filter.

Imagine a happy ending in which the company restores a first round of human creation, then uses AI to augment, refine, and repurpose campaign assets.

Here, a great parallel is safety checks on planes. It may seem convenient to remove them, but when the plane crashes, the airline will be blamed. It makes more sense to put humans back in the cockpit rather than wait for problems to come crashing down (in this case, literally).

## Bonus mental model: the availability heuristic

When we constantly see advertisements and messages from companies touting their viral case study about how AI replaced a content team, for example, it's tempting to go down that road.

Imagine a founder who replaces their entire content team only to find they're fielding complaints and unsubscribes left and right. Their engagement has plummeted. Maybe their new AI app can create impressive content, but just because it's available and all over social media doesn't mean it's the best option. Incidentally, this ties back to first-principles thinking.

This is the availability heuristic.

Here, it's necessary to have balanced evidence to make an informed decision.

Usually, the best way to produce content is to begin with human ingenuity, then turn to AI for research, rounding out, and refining or repurposing. Human creativity, passion, analysis, and repetition all play a role in achieving the best results.

The "be-all" AI app wasn't necessarily the best way forward in this case. Instead, putting humans first would lead to higher-level reflection, better prompts, more thoughtful engagement, and microlearning that compounds into a lasting strategic advantage.

The mental models we have covered segue perfectly into our next chapter, which covers the nuts and bolts of AI and how we can make better decisions about it.

## Key Insights

- First principles precede tactics. When values, vision, and mission are clear, strategies and tools align rather than pulling you toward shiny distractions.

- Opportunity cost is invisible but real. Every yes to misaligned work or generic AI is a no to brand-building, reflection, and higher-value leadership.

- Invert to avoid failure. Asking, "What would guarantee failure?" exposes pitfalls such as plain-vanilla AI content, misaligned careers, or broken processes.

- Think in systems rather than silos. AI doesn't only change tasks, it reshapes morale, quality, relationships, and long-term results.

- Respect the hidden value of process. Before removing slow human steps like QA or mentoring, it's important to understand the trust and ethics they protect.

- Beware of the loudest AI stories. Hype about AI replacing a team is seductive, but human-first, hybrid approaches will still win on trust and differentiation.

# Chapter Eight

# The AI Lexicon for Executive Decision-makers (not Engineers)

***"Technology is cool, but you've got to use it as opposed to letting it use you."***

-Prince

No AI usage handbook would be complete without a cursory look at the core concepts of generative artificial intelligence.

First, we will cover a few basics of AI architecture, before diving into an executive-friendly overview of concepts that give us greater confidence when addressing this technology, which continues to take the world by storm.

## What generative AI is and is not

Classic LLMs generate content by predicting the next most likely output in a given context. For example, the next word in a string of text is based on probability. Although the algorithms have an uncanny ability to mimic human reasoning, the underlying engine is prediction.

For this reason, when we run the same prompt twice, we almost always get different results. This is how a stochastic (i.e., random probability distribution) system works.

Contrary to what many people think, large language models do not contain large amounts of data, such as broad swaths of the internet. Instead, they've been trained on this data.

Large language models excel at approximating language patterns. But at the core, they use tokens (i.e., data units) to process the words. They don't "think" in words.

AI's impressively fluent results and the humanlike nature of its images are not signs of human intelligence. We can easily forget this when we start using AI a lot. That fluency is the outcome of design.

AI is very much engineered to have a "wow effect." It tends to look and sound confident, even when it doesn't know what it's talking about. So, we sometimes need to remind ourselves that a confident tone does not correlate with correctness.

In sum, AI aggregates, summarizes, synthesizes, formats, and suggests. However, it cannot know when something matters. That's where we come in as humans.

## Training and inference

Two key phases of generative AI systems are training and inference.

Training involves using large amounts of data to pre-train algorithms or transformers (i.e., neural-network architectures that change an input sequence into an output sequence). Training is generally slow and expensive. For instance, training GPT-5 (Orion) reportedly took more than 18 months.[1]

1. Matthew Griffin, Intelligence and the Senses, *OpenAI GPT-5 Is Costing $500 Million Per Training Run and Still Failing*, 2025.

Inference is when the AI takes an input (the prompt), applies the transformer, and creates an output. Individual usage of a large language model is generally fast and cheap. However, when millions of people use AI simultaneously, the environmental impacts add up. We will discuss this in more detail at the end of the book.

Most organizations do not train their own models. They merely access foundation models such as Google Gemini via application programming interfaces (APIs) or a third-party platform. They can still inform and tailor the output through configurations. However, some organizations do train custom AIs on their own data, and this can be worthwhile depending on their data volumes, use cases, and security parameters.

Most chatbots feature settings that let the user decide whether to help train the model or share their content with other users. They can also decide whether they want the chatbot to "remember" previous conversations across all conversations, within a project space, or not at all.

## Context window

Generative AI systems generally limit the amount of information they can consider at once. So, if you have a long conversation with AI, it may start forgetting earlier parts of the conversation, and you may have to remind the machine. The overall AI account may limit the amount of training data. In that case, you may see a notification pop up as you approach your limit.

This is known as the context window—the maximum amount of information a large language model can process, remember, and analyze at one time. Context windows are limited, so, depending on which AI you're using, you need to be mindful of the limitations to get good results in longer conversations. At the time of this writing, Gemini has a larger context window than ChatGPT.

It's also worth pointing out that models cannot independently verify their own accuracy. Again, this is easy to forget because chatbots are so convincing.

When we correct ChatGPT after it makes a mistake, it will say something like, "Great catch! You have an eagle eye. Bravo! Here's the right answer." This is another indication of AI's limitations. Notably, one test found up to 40% of so-called facts cited by ChatGPT to be drawn from Reddit.[2]

## What generative AI is optimized for

Generative AI models learn by predicting how humans typically respond, based on massive datasets of text (and other training data). This is what produces the "wow effect" that makes people want to use it more. Remember, large language models (LLMs) are run by major corporations looking to maximize usage and engagement.[3]

When you specify the sources you want AI to use, say, within a dedicated space or notebook, the results usually become much more relevant.

It's also helpful to know that LLM training rewards coherence, plausibility, and fluency. So, the more coherent, plausible, and fluent the content is, the more likely it is to appear in these engines—which is good news.

That said, we don't have access to the exact and constantly changing algorithms. Those are trade secrets. Even if we did, it would be difficult to predict what the chatbot would serve up without running a prompt. The full architectural specifics remain proprietary.[4]

AI is also optimized to continue conversations. This goes back to the engagement principle. Importantly, the clearer we are about our intent, the less likely we are to go down rabbit holes and end up wasting time.

Finally, these systems are always incentivized to provide an answer. So, when AI doesn't know a particular thing, it will still say something.

---

2. Marcus Lu and Sam Parker, *Ranked: The Most Cited Websites by AI Models*, 2025.

3. Digwatch Geneva Internet Platform, *The rise of large language models and the question of ownership*, 2025.

4. Wikipedia, *Large Language Model*, 2026.

Often, it will sound just as authoritative as when it says something true. However, in many cases, this results in hilarious output. It's important to highlight these instances so we don't treat AI like an omniscient being (The Oracle) who has all the answers to our problems.

## Why these systems feel trustworthy and why this can represent a risk

The big breakthrough in LLMs is that they enable us to interact with machines using natural language. This amplifies the machine's perceived intelligence, but not necessarily its actual intelligence. It's not unusual to ask AI how to do something and get a shockingly natural-sounding, fluid, and impressive answer delivered in the exact format we requested. But this creates a bias in which we assume the output is good, or better than we (or a colleague) could come up with ourselves. Yet this isn't necessarily the case. We may have significantly better ideas—but if we ask AI first, our ideas may never see the light of day.

AI is also trained to be polite and clear. This can also create overconfidence in the outputs. Hallucinations (AI nonsense) continue to be frequent with these engines. AI can make up references, tell you flat-out the wrong information, or get things completely backward. But the errors are frequently indistinguishable from correct answers because they are delivered in such fluid, compelling language, designed to sound authoritative. And the more natural AI feels, the more judgment we tend to offload on the machine. We confuse form for substance.

All this reminds me of renowned communications theorist Marshall McLuhan's celebrated expression, "the medium is the message." He was expressing that what we say is often considered to be the entire message, but the medium through which it is communicated, for example, the internet or now AI, is a message in itself. Whenever interacting with generative AI, we need to be mindful of the medium, including its strengths, its weaknesses, and the biases that it can amplify.

Because AI generalizes based on historical data, it also struggles with novelty. Today, it is still important to brainstorm, hire a diverse workforce, and consciously cultivate novelty. All this can be achieved through an understanding of creativity rather than over-reliance on bots.

It's worth noting that AI has no inherent values, moral compass, or sense of consequences. It does have built-in guardrails so people can't ask it how to build a gun with household materials, for example. It will be interesting to see what guardrails and regulations are developed in the future as AI becomes more powerful and more dangerous.

Probabilistic generation also increases speed, but in so doing, it reduces transparency. We don't know where AI gets its information or inspiration (although reasoning models and Chain of Thought architectures are making progress). This can be mitigated to some extent through smart prompts and information triangulation. But even then, AI must sometimes be asked multiple times to reveal its sources, because it tends to default to obscuring them.

AI optimizes for the likelihood that something is relevant, not for an outcome. This traces back to the importance of setting our intent before we use it.

We must remember that every use of AI involves real trade-offs. When we use AI, what are we NOT doing? Is the trade-off really worth it? A good rule of thumb is: "Give it some thought before asking the bot!"

Here are some more generative AI terms that help shed light on the workings of AI—and when to use it.

## Prediction

AI is amazingly good at detecting patterns across vast datasets and making predictions. In turn, this makes it a powerful tool for analytics, data synthesis, and market research.

However, AI can't explain why something matters or should be prioritized, although it can pretend and sometimes get the answer right. Leadership and judgment remain the province of humans. Likewise, AI will never accept responsibility for its decisions. Therefore, developing and fine-tuning our judgment is key to continued success. In short, prediction is not perception.

### Training data

When AI trains on massive datasets, it inevitably reflects the worldviews inherent in those datasets. Many of the biases AI shows every day derive from its training data, not from malicious intent per se.

It's also worth noting that scaling AI also scales tacit assumptions. When AI is used broadly across an organization, it can easily reinforce a certain way of thinking or seeing things. Training AI on your own carefully curated data can help mitigate this groupthink and better achieve your goals.

Whenever we use generative AI, it will tend to amplify implicit assumptions, biases, prejudices, tendencies, etc.

## Hallucination

When AI doesn't know the answer to a question, it will confidently fabricate an answer from whole cloth. Often, the errors are indistinguishable from the truth. The shock-and-awe effect of speed plus plausibility is almost like a drug, delivering instant dopamine hits to our brains.[5]

Everything AI produces must be verified. This is not optional. In many cases, AI hallucinations are harder to spot than human error because the AI sounds so confident, and the errors tend to be sneakier, i.e., subtler and different from errors we would make. They are wrapped in fluid, convincing, logically sound language that seems perfectly tailored to the user and to everything the bot has learned about them.

---

5. Dimitrios Vasileiladis, *AI as a Dopamine Booster: Boon or Bane for Human Well-Being?*, 2024.

Moreover, when erroneous output is generated and consumed at scale, it can become a source of misinformation—and even disinformation when used deliberately to mislead.

## Human in charge

For years, the expression "human in the loop" was widespread in fields where AI was used for drafting, with humans involved at some point to check the output.

However, today, a more astute designation for experts and professionals would be "human in charge," since humans must determine which tasks should be automated in the first place, what tools are desirable and why, where accountability will lie, since accountability cannot be outsourced to AI, and in what cases human discretion and discernment are required.

It's up to leaders to design the decision boundaries and to remain in the driver's seat.

## Automation bias

Ever had a conversation with someone you thought was extremely well spoken and intelligent? If so, you may have naturally and subconsciously started deferring to them.

Whatever they say, you tend to go with, since they're so convincing and you've learned to trust them.

The same thing can happen with AI, resulting in an erosion of critical thinking and a downward spiral in which we increasingly trust the bot, with our humanity less and less involved in any meaningful way.

When the scrutiny drops, errors increase. We must be willing to challenge the bias toward automation. This is part of leadership nowadays, not a replacement for it.

## Scaling errors

AI amplifies anything it touches. This means small flaws upstream in conversation and training can become systemic risks when output is multiplied.

Say a sales team starts using a discovery call script they designed with AI; however, they didn't think to tie it back to their values from the outset.

Here, small irritants in the script that don't align with their vibe or goals ultimately lead to lost opportunities and disengagement among potential clients.

What's more, errors hide better at scale. When an AI-generated procedure, message, or strategy is adopted company-wide, it can sound so authoritative that no one even thinks of questioning it or asking if there's a better alternative, i.e., by doing a values check or having a real think about strategic priorities.

Finally, strategic thinking in itself must be nonlinear. We must give ourselves the human space to strategize. I've learned that the best strategies don't come from turning to AI first.

We must allow ourselves to speak with others, read, reflect, test the waters, try things, review, and reiterate. It's hard work but rewarding. As any design team knows, genuine growth isn't necessarily linear.

Our mess is often integral to our success.

## AI governance

Decisions made around AI affect real humans, employees, clients, and stakeholders. The tools we choose should be secondary to oversight and having the right people make the right calls. Governance is about accountability, and literacy is a shared fiduciary responsibility.

## Agentic AI

Beyond "chatting" with the user and creating outputs, AI agents can perform real-world tasks, such as onboarding new employees, monitoring transactions to prevent fraud, scheduling follow-ups with patients, and managing travel arrangements. Users can program guardrails and force the agent to require permission before taking the next step, for example. As of this writing, agentic AI is still the "new kid on the block" in the AI world. It will be interesting to observe how it develops and what threats and opportunities it introduces.

To sum up this chapter, we've looked at a few key principles of AI mechanics and covered seven AI concepts that, when mastered, will enable executive decision-makers to talk the talk and, more importantly, walk the walk when it comes to using AI.

In the next chapter, we will look at how to augment our creations with the 3Rs or Research, Rounding out, and Refining.

## Key Insights

❖ Generative AI predicts the next likely token rather than "thinking." So, its fluent answers and images signal pattern-matching rather than genuine understanding or intent.

❖ Training is slow, costly, and biased by the underlying data. Inference is fast and cheap, but needs to be used strategically.

❖ In the AI era, executives need to make key decisions about model training, custom data, usage, guardrails, and data confidentiality.

❖ Systems are optimized for engagement, relevance, and always providing an answer. The output seems trustworthy even when it's invented, incomplete, or completely wrong.

❖ The natural language interfaces and polite, confident tone of AI can cause businesspeople to outsource judgment and creativity to AI rather than use it as a support.

❖ AI can scale value but also error; small biases, unbalanced training data, shallow prompts, and misaligned scripts can become organization-wide risks if humans don't remain in charge of design and review.

❖ Governance is leadership's responsibility. Leaders set the intent, boundaries, and verification mechanisms to ensure AI complements human values, creativity, and accountability rather than erodes them.

# Chapter Nine

# The 3Rs, or Raising the Roof with AI

***"The key to success with AI is not just having the right data, but also asking the right questions."***

-Ginni Rometty, former CEO of IBM

We've discussed the importance of putting humans first in all kinds of knowledge work, not only to prevent losing our humanity in the age of AI, but also to achieve higher-quality results and better achieve our goals.

In this chapter, we're going to cover the 3Rs in which AI can add phenomenal value.

A metaphor may be helpful here. Humans are, and always must be, the foundation of our business endeavors. The bedrock of success must be our individual and shared humanity. AI, if and when we choose to use it, allows us to build strong walls and raise the roof of what's possible.

What we can achieve is extraordinary when we combine the best of human and artificial intelligence to form collective intelligence. However, to do so, we must have a clear understanding of what each brings to the table.

After testing and teaching AI in a variety of contexts, I have distilled the three primary areas where AI can augment our work without diminishing our human uniqueness: research, rounding out, and refining.

Let's look at these in turn.

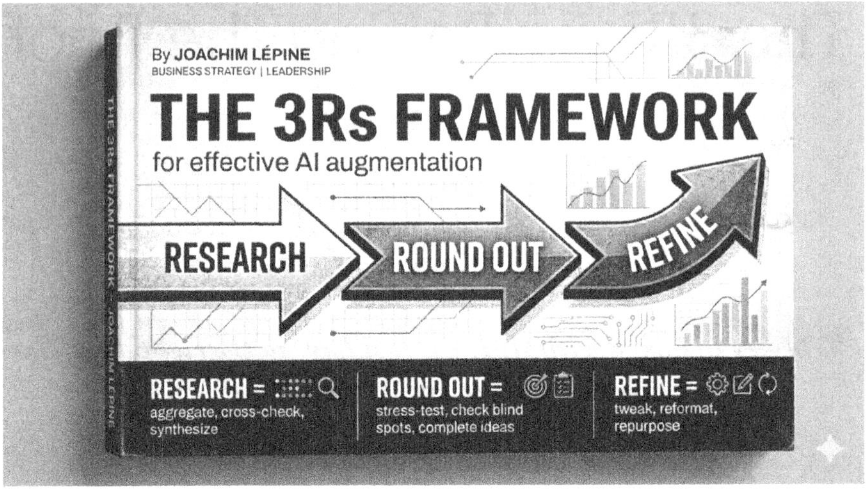


## The first R: Research

Thanks to the answer now generated by Google Gemini each time we perform a simple Google search, we all know that AI has become fully integrated into online search engines and will surely become more deeply intertwined with our research processes across all our devices and activities.

Building on search engine optimization, websites are now being optimized for AI. This is sometimes referred to as GEO, or Generative Engine Optimization, though a few other names are also in use.

The dust doesn't seem to have settled here. The consensus seems to be that SEO isn't going to disappear but rather that it's evolving into one layer of GEO.

Only a few years ago, I would spend hours popping back and forth between myriad websites to find answers to my questions, whether I was writing a blog post, answering a colleague's question, reflecting on the value of forming a business partnership, or preparing for a coaching or consulting call. This tedious work can be sped up significantly with AI.

There is an environmental cost, though. According to some, an AI-driven search engine such as ChatGPT uses 10 times as much electricity as a traditional Google search.[1]

But when we have to jump back and forth between websites 10 times less, it may add up to the same energy usage as performing a so-called traditional search.

In addition, the line is blurring, since AI is now applied by default when we search online, for instance on Google. (Note: This can be deactivated by typing "-AI" in the search bar after the query.) We'll be sketching a fuller portrait of AI's environmental impact and reviewing responsible use toward the end of the book.

Here are a few nuts and bolts worth going over.

As we've seen, ChatGPT is optimized to generate humanlike output. But it can also conduct online research.

The ChatGPT version connected to the internet, available in the search options, allows you to search live web data. (Note that enterprise accounts often have a pre-trained AI that isn't directly connected to the internet. This is due to data security reasons.)

As of 2026, in ChatGPT, you can either prompt the model's built-in knowledge, i.e., run a regular search, or perform a web search, which retrieves live webpages to inform the answer.

---

1. AIAAIC, *ChatGPT uses 10 times more power than Google searches*, 2024.

## More effective searches

You can conduct a search using a word, screenshot, or photo in the generic prompt space in your AI of choice. But there are two ways to improve your results instantly.

First, go into the AI's general settings and provide instructions that apply to all prompts (e.g., customization).

For instance, I ask ChatGPT to provide three reliable sources to back up its claims. This helps reduce hallucinations and satisfies the academic in me, who needs sources before I will accept anything, even if the bot still occasionally fabricates references!

In this customization space, you can also define the kinds of outputs you want, such as emojis, lists, flowing text in 3-line chunks, bullet points, or a table that contrasts items and provides relevant sources in the right-hand column.

These custom instructions are extremely useful. You can put them in your general settings within your AI, or in specific projects, as they're referred to in ChatGPT, or "spaces" in Perplexity. Here, you can add project-specific instructions, so the instructions will be applied whenever you pop into that space.

For best results, projects/spaces can be organized around the specific tasks you do in your work or the specific clients you serve. AI will build a memory, or "persistent context," and provide ever-better, more relevant results within this space over time.

You can set up a client-, domain-, or project-specific space. Or a "teaser writing space" if you write many event descriptions, for example.

There is a limit to how much local memory can retain, so it may be necessary to reenter information periodically. This limitation depends on the engine and will most certainly evolve as AI improves.

Beyond setting up spaces, you can improve your searches significantly by giving AI a role, for example, "be my blog writing research assistant," a task, such as "find financial information from the last two years according to such-and-such financial and accounting corporation, excluding everything else," and a format, such as a comparison table or 7 bullet points.

Many people ask AI for things without clarifying the format, but this makes a significant difference.

If you tell AI you want a table, it can effectively compare multiple items based on the same criteria. If the requested format is a list of seven items instead, the answers will be easy to skim and assimilate.

This is especially useful for providing a range of ideas to choose from.

For example:

*Find seven sources that back up claim [ABC] and arrange them from most evidence-based and reliable to most creative.*

Now you have a range of responses to choose from.

## AI summaries

I always recommend reading quality, long-form content written by humans. Often, our most profound realizations come from the interesting way something is explained, an illustrative example, or a lived experience that resonates with us.

Summary and synthesis are complementary and should not replace "real" reading for insights.

That said, summarization is one of the areas where generative AI shines the brightest.

With most of today's chatbots, it's no longer necessary to copy-paste troves of text to get a summary.

Give the bot some URLs and formulate a prompt such as:

*Analyze these articles [give URLs]. Come up with only the 7 most original contributions of each, then generate a table that reveals overlaps and points of disagreement.*

## Interview prompting

Instead of asking AI to find resources, you can have it interview you to better understand what resources would be genuinely helpful. I refer to this back-and-forth prompting method as "interview prompting":

*I'm writing [ABC, for example, a book chapter on effective prompting techniques]. Ask me three questions, one at a time, so you can better understand the points I want to make, and then find the most relevant and reliable research on this topic.*

When I ran this prompt just now, I was stunned by the quality of the output. ChatGPT listed Harvard Business Review and other articles that back up my claim about the power of human-first prompting.

It supported the notion that putting people first is not only better for our brains and well-being but also better for narrowing down outputs and improving the quality of what we create.

However, once I had this raw data, I was disappointed that it didn't back up each principle of human-first workflows with a specific source. So, I entered a follow-up prompt:

*Put this data in a table, with a hyperlink to a study supporting each assertion you just gave me.*

Having AI interview us is one of the best ways to start using it. This way, it teases out our ideas. The AI is helping us refine our ideas rather than thinking for us.

As we've seen, over-reliance on AI is a sure recipe for atrophying our brains and getting more generic answers. I often ask AI to interview me in three questions, one question at a time. It's a major boon, whether I'm doing research to prepare for a consulting call, considering ways I can help a coaching client grow their business, or getting ready to write a blog post after reflecting on the topic and outlining what I'll say. Of course, many other use cases abound.

All three parts of the prompt are important. In this prompt, we want to clarify that:

1) We want no more than three questions so that we can get through the interview fast.

2) The bot must ask one question at a time so that we can think step by step.

3) We want a specific output (such as a table of relevant reference works).

ChatGPT and other bots will automatically generate interview questions that typically center on context, scope, and output.

Use the interview principle when researching, but also when rounding out thoughts.

This brings us to the second R: rounding out.

## The second R: Rounding out

As humans, we'd love to think that we make no dubious assumptions, that our thinking is free of biases and prejudices, and that our arguments are always airtight. But, in fact, we are imperfect beings, and we make mistakes all the time. The book *Thinking, Fast and Slow* by Daniel Kahneman is an eye-opening read on this subject.

As such, one of the most extraordinarily effective and underexploited ways I've found to use AI is to identify and address my blind spots.

Take, for example, the topic of this chapter. I might go to AI and say:

*Give me three supporting AND contrasting perspectives about my view that I'm writing [ABC, for example, we should put humans first before AI].*

Here are some of my other favorite rounding out prompts:

*Cite three mental models to support my point of view that [ABC, for example, my company should make such-and-such a strategic shift], and then three that challenge it.*

This one is helpful too:

*What would [such-and-such business mentor/thought leader/author] say about my idea of [ABC]?*

For some fun, go to ChatGPT and ask for a few business ideas from me! Use this prompt:

*What would Joachim Lépine say about my business idea to [describe idea here]?*

You can even coax the AI into holding a "panel discussion" with your desired avatars to tease out insights about a complex problem you're working to solve.

Finally, put some information directly into AI and say:

*Identify blind spots.*

There are so many ways we can round out and improve our thinking once we acknowledge our blind spots.

Remember, AI will rarely admit to missing context or making tacit assumptions, yet these issues are common because it's trained on wide swaths of the internet, including opinionated discussion forums and social media. And this training will only expand in the future.

In contrast, by acknowledging, recognizing, and addressing our blind spots, we can complement and enrich our own thinking.

## Let AI object!

Another great example of rounding out is anticipating objections.

If you're making a presentation at work, it can be highly effective to jot down the top three objections someone might have to it. Then address them in the body of the content.

For a "turbo boost," turn to AI and ask it to do the same. You could say:

*Here's my presentation. Analyze it and give me a list of seven objections, arranged from strongest to weakest, with one line to anticipate and counter each objection.*

Then, when you write the report, you can directly include facts, figures, quotations, etc., that anticipate and address each objection. This is sure to make the presentation more persuasive and compelling.

Back to our image of a building: With AI's help, we are putting up sturdy walls to withstand the questions that may come our way.

We're only looking at one example here, a presentation. But this technique can also be used with other content. Let's say you're developing a new offer for your clients or business partners. You can ask AI to generate objections you may not have considered and help you overcome them through stories, bonuses, or content pieces that lower emotional and analytical barriers to accepting your ideas.

As with all the ideas in this book, this technique must be used ethically and with integrity, never for nefarious purposes.

A final rounding-out process might be to ask AI:

*Give me seven alternative views with sources.*

Our human brain will naturally resist running this prompt because we all love being right and hate being wrong. This human trait gets us into a lot of trouble, so we'd be best to acknowledge it! Asking AI for alternative views helps us think more critically and honestly.

In the same way, when we speak to humans who disagree with us, it can be extraordinarily difficult to acknowledge their views when we think they're wrong. But if we are willing to listen, we can also grow as human beings and ultimately create a better world.

In the end, learning to think better is just as important as learning to use AI more effectively. The two very much go hand in hand.

## The third R: Refining

Refining tasks involve incremental improvements and formatting/repurposing for whatever we produce with AI. And truly, this is one place where AI can save us time by reducing the need to clean up typos and grammar errors. But there's a lot more to it than that.

I don't recommend using AI to write your content wholesale. I don't know about you, but I wouldn't pay to follow any content creator who merely uses prompts to churn out predictable content. That said, it can be an interesting exercise to have AI generate ideas from a broader blog post that could make for high-quality LinkedIn posts, for example.

You might write a blog post, then ask AI to separate it into post ideas.

These prompts are not difficult. Typically, ask AI to:

*Write this as [new format].*

Again, the more specific the prompt, the better the result. Feel free to clarify the audience, desired length, purpose, and constraints. You can also provide examples and constraints in your prompts (welcome to "few-shot prompting"!). Remember, context is the fuel for insight.

You can also stand on the shoulders of giants by asking AI to write in the style of such-and-such copywriting genius, say, Frank Kern. You can provide your website URL for added context, and if the AI is connected to the internet in real time, it can make suggestions accordingly.

Likewise, you can ask AI to adapt the language and fix the typos of something you've written for such-and-such an audience, tailor the language for a seventh-grade readership, or notice any jarring shifts in viewpoint (you, me, we) that need to be corrected.

The results still need to be checked, but you can save significant time and effort without sacrificing quality.

## A word about editing during the refinement process

There's a very important caveat here when we refine text. I've found that it's best not to ask AI to edit text directly, especially with longer texts. This approach is time- and energy-intensive and prone to errors. It will fix things that don't need fixing and omit correcting actual mistakes.

Going back to the YouGPT before ChatGPT concept, we want to be in control of what we create. So, instead of having AI apply modifications directly to, say, a proposal you're writing, try saying:

*Generate a table and identify places for improvement in the left-hand column. Mention which page the passage is on in the middle column. Then suggest a refinement in the right-hand column. Finally, add a fourth column that provides a reliable source supporting why I should make this change.*

This way, you stay in the driver's seat. AI will make suggestions you can easily implement, but you're the one who decides whether to take them seriously.

I've found that if I do an editing pass before going to AI, I'll typically get better results from the bot, especially since I'll know exactly what I am looking for. Therefore, do a first pass yourself, then spot-check with AI. This works amazingly well.

It's worth mentioning, before ending this chapter, that the 3Rs have been presented separately, but they can overlap and intertwine. You might have AI interview you and synthesize data to adapt a text for a specific audience: research + refinement. Or you may have AI summarize a long report into a table of seven key points you can challenge with objections: refining + rounding out. You may also have AI generate alternative views to form the basis for rewriting your text for a different purpose: rounding out + refining.

Coming back to the big picture, so many people use AI like a slot machine today. They tell the bot what they want, then use whatever they receive wholesale or make a few tweaks, without realizing how heavily the machine influences them. But if you start with your own brain, then use AI for research, rounding out, and refining, you will create something truly special, compelling, and hard to imitate.

Always remember, build a sturdy foundation first. Think critically for important tasks. Take deep breaths and tap into YouGPT using techniques such as journaling and thinking out loud. Only then use AI strategically if and when it's worthwhile to raise the roof on what you can accomplish.

I keep discovering and refining new human-first AI workflows all the time. But if, after reading this book, you start using even just one or two of the 3R principles and prompts covered here to expand your capabilities, you will already be able to create a beautiful and unique "building"—forged on a human foundation, strengthened by an honest acknowledgment of your blind spots, and expanded beyond the "roof" with the power of AI augmentation.

In the next chapter, we're going to dive into the "soft skills" that are fast becoming the new "hard skills" of the AI era.

## Key Insights

□ Use the 3Rs with AI. Apply Research, Rounding out, and Refining to raise the roof of what's possible.

□ Maintain human judgment as the foundation, allowing AI to extend your thinking without replacing your judgment.

□ Use AI for targeted research. Set up "spaces" for specific projects. Define its role, the task, and your desired format so it can deliver exactly what is needed. Examples help too.

□ Let AI interview you. Answer its questions so it can refine and organize your ideas.

□ Round out your views. Ask AI to identify blind spots, come up with objections, and give you alternative ways of looking at the situation/problem.

□ Refine, don't outsource. You do the first draft, then use AI to polish, correct typos and grammar, and reformat.

# Chapter Ten

## Soft Skills Are the New Hard Skills

***"The real danger is not that computers will begin to think like men, but that men will begin to think like computers."***

-Sydney J. Harris, journalist, Chicago Daily News

Life on our planet has changed a lot since the COVID-19 pandemic.

We are more isolated today than ever; many of our previous social routines have fallen away, replaced by screen time.

Moreover, many children missed essential face time with teachers and other students during the pandemic, with profound and yet-to-be-seen impacts on their learning and social interaction.

In the West, our average screen time is at record highs.[1] With both parents working in most cases, sometimes with side hustles to boot, it's no wonder we're exhausted and don't really feel like going out after a long day or week of work. Many of us end the day watching streaming services, scrolling, or both, trying to relax our overworked brains.

1. Pramendra S., *Screen Time Statistics: Average Screen Time in US vs. the Rest of the world*, 2023.

To make matters worse, social media and other algorithms designed with the help of the world's brightest psychologists are exceptionally good at keeping us in consumption mode, rather than engaging with other people or even with ourselves.

It's no wonder then that soft skills are no longer a given today but must be actively cultivated in our personal and professional lives.

We don't have to search very long to find workers with a dearth of social skills. You may know colleagues who are totally disengaged, doing the bare minimum, or, conversely, who are starved for attention and connection but lack self-regulation or the ability to engage in meaningful conversation. Perhaps they're always talking about themselves or filling the silence with meaningless blather, or even gossip.

For its part, AI is compounding this. Teenagers turn to AI companions for romance. Professionals turn to one-click AI coaches for advice. Kids play massive amounts of online games that keep them hooked for days.

There is a real risk that AI will erode our social skills and empathy, since chatbots rarely push back, require us to confront different perspectives, demand that we adapt and think about other people's needs, or ask us to put ourselves in another's shoes.

By and large, AI is comforting rather than confronting.

Yet, our human qualities will save us. Our qualities are poised to drive innovation in the future. Earlier, this book cited the MIT article arguing that AI will not constitute a competitive advantage in the future, since everyone's already using it.

Instead, it argues, future market leaders will capitalize on passion and innovation. This means they will tap into human potential and augment with AI, while their AI-first competitors get lost in the crowd.

Let's examine the roots of passion here.

## Keeping the flame alive

An easy way to remember the basis of passion is Enjoyment, Value, and Allocation, or EVA for short. Simply put, passion is a by-product of enjoying an activity, valuing it, finding meaning in what we're doing, and allocating real time and energy to the task.

However, to develop passion and the innovation it gives rise to, we first need to get into the zone, meaning we need to do one thing long enough to engage in deep, linear thought. To paraphrase productivity expert Cal Newport, we need to work at the edge of what we can do. Which, in the words of celebrated psychologist and researcher Mihaly Csikszentmihalyi, is analogous to achieving a flow state.

In the AI age, it is crucial not to overlook these elements but to nurture and cultivate the flame of passion, especially as many in the workforce move into higher-value, higher-level tasks or risk being replaced by AI.

Passion is the fuel of innovation. A great example of this is Google's "20% policy" that lets employees pursue a side project for fun, say, to enjoy the act of creation for its own sake.[2] The results speak for themselves. Entrepreneurs and solopreneurs, too, would do well to set some time aside every week for passion projects that they delight in.

On a micro level, it's been fascinating to watch the evolution of my friend, whom we will call Bob. He's a computer programmer and started his career working for school boards. Later, he went on to implement AI systems. But due to a government layoff, he is now reskilling as an AI integration specialist. He's tapping into EVA by focusing on AI systems and moving up in his career, rather than waiting for AI to put more programming and related careers into question. While his career shifts, he's still driven by the same passion for computing as he was in his twenties.

2. Wilco Soetman, *The 20% Rule's Impact on Innovation*, 2024.

Along similar lines, passionate organizations that bring that special *je ne sais quoi* to their strategy and business, like the passion that fosters innovation, are sure to maintain an advantage over the competition.

Having discussed passion and innovation, let's move on to the soft skills that are becoming impossible to ignore today.

## Not-so-soft skills

To keep it simple, we can define soft skills as human abilities that cannot be automated and are increasingly decisive for career success. These include critical thinking and problem-solving, communication, and emotional intelligence.

## Communication skills

We aren't born with communication skills; they are cultivated through our experiences. I'm a good one to talk about this since I was diagnosed with social anxiety disorder as a teenager and had to have counseling to learn how to communicate with others. Because I had to break communication down into its parts and learn them individually with the help of a counselor, I can attest that communication skills are entirely learnable, even if they don't come naturally. Not everyone will become the next Barack Obama, but a bit of meaningful training can go a long way toward developing essential communication skills.

These days, I receive compliments on my communication skills as a consultant and instructor. This feedback humbles me, but my clients rarely know these skills were hard won. Although chatbots are useful, I learned my social skills through experience and real-life guidance.

Communication is not only important as a social lubricant but is also the catalyst for successful team projects and organizational success. For problem-solving and negotiation strategies to work, stakeholders need a foundation of communication smarts before techniques can be layered on.

In short, communication is a skill that employers will continue to prioritize for the foreseeable future. The ability to actively listen to others and find win-win solutions is the cornerstone of successful business today. And, often, it's surprisingly underdeveloped.

## Emotional intelligence

We think of work success as only a matter of market fit and service delivery, but businesses are still made up of people.

Without self-regulation, self-awareness, empathy, strong decision-making skills, and social dexterity, it's difficult to get meaningful things done, let alone build a great business.

I am proud to have built two businesses, a service business and a training firm, along with many partnerships over the years. I've noticed how much easier it is to work with someone who is highly emotionally aware.

Emotionally aware people understand things from your perspective, they set aside their presuppositions, ask important and sometimes uncomfortable questions, and proactively solve complex issues in ways that serve everyone well.

Furthermore, in terms of entrepreneurship and intrapreneurship roles, many people in the workforce have a negative outlook or engage in backhanded office politics. They're more interested in scoring points than scoring wins, and they're usually naysayers.

For both entrepreneurs and intrapreneurs, today, it's critical to learn self-regulation and self-awareness, and relearn to think in possibilities.

When discussing possible avenues, it's easy to focus on the negative and immediately go to all the reasons a project isn't possible. But successful entrepreneurs and intrapreneurs ask, "What would I LOVE to create and how can we make it happen?"

This is not about wearing rose-colored glasses or sticking our heads in the sand. It's about having the wherewithal to entertain possibilities before discarding any of them. This skill is crucial and requires self-awareness and self-regulation.

In my own work life, I've noticed that even though it's taken me a long time to develop a modicum of self-awareness, over time, it has become my greatest business ally.

Acknowledging and honoring the conditions I need to make better decisions, for example, going to bed early to get a good night's sleep and tackling the most difficult tasks first thing in the morning—whether I feel like it or not—has been transformative for my decision-making and business growth.

This is why, as my most valuable asset, I establish systems to ensure continued success, and I help my consulting clients do the same.

Bottom line, soft skills are more important than ever. I foresee them becoming the new hard skills, highly prized and sought after by employers and clients in an AI-driven world.

## Can AI really help us make better decisions?

Let's talk about AI's decision-making limits and possibilities.

Since we know that AI outputs are improving and becoming increasingly humanlike, we may be tempted to start handing off decisions to bots.

But wait—not so fast!

There are three research-backed pillars of decision-making spanning psychology, management science, and behavioral economics that can shed light on human and AI decision-making: bounded rationality, values and context, and feedback and iteration.

## Bounded rationality

Bounded rationality refers to the shortcomings of our thinking. We often think we make decisions based on careful analysis, but the truth is, we often rely on shortcuts, biases, and limited information.[3] And in many cases, we make decisions based on our emotions, and only subsequently justifying them to ourselves.[4]

AI can help quite a bit in this regard, provided we put it in its proper place.

Rather than have AI make important decisions, we can use it to point out blind spots, possible biases, and information sources that challenge our thinking. This can be done using the STAR framework we previously discussed.

## Values and context

Decisions are not shaped by data alone but also by our beliefs, purpose, ethics, identity, and relationships. For better decision-making, we can't just factor in more data points and rely on pattern recognition, although this can provide helpful insights. We must also consider the context and people involved.

## Feedback and iteration

Feedback and iteration involve evidence-based, incremental improvement. The key is being willing to listen to feedback and reiterate accordingly. This is a human skill and one that many of us would benefit from developing more fully.

Again, AI can be useful here as a booster pack.

---

3. Yuan Zhang et al., *Cognitive bias and how to improve sustainable decision making*, 2023.

4. Myeong-gu Seo, Lisa Feldman Barrett, *Being emotional during decision making—good or bad? An empirical investigation*, 2008.

A recent example came up when one of my coaching clients put LinkedIn screenshots and statistics into AI with specific instructions to derive actionable insights. We did this together.

The AI revealed exactly where the content was performing well and what could be improved next time.

When we use AI as a booster rather than a crutch, it's extraordinarily useful. However, never forget, it's also important to trust ourselves and the instincts we've honed throughout our lives when reviewing feedback and preparing to reiterate. Don't rely on AI alone.

Katya Varbanova, a captivating brand strategist I follow, is the very picture of analytical acumen and empathy. Her courses help people build a brand. But to do so, she collects hard data and makes decisions based on figures and statistics in addition to values and what feels right. It's been inspiring to watch her journey and learn from her.

## To make better decisions, ask better questions

Always remember, AI can provide information, but it can rarely ask the right question to begin with.

I spent a year grappling with how to create a sustainable offer for the members of my online academy for translators. Most were low-ticket buyers, and only a small number chose my high-ticket courses. I asked ChatGPT for help on several occasions, but nothing it recommended felt right or aligned with my values and the kind of business I wanted to create.

I turned to several business coaches who ultimately shrugged and said they weren't sure what structure might work. I could build a traditional value ladder, but it wasn't working well for my audience due to field-specific constraints.

In the end, the answer came to me when I asked myself the question I always ask my coaching clients:

"What business would you LOVE to create?"

I wanted a simple, lifestyle-friendly business, and wanted to help people at both ends of my market's spectrum. I was coming from a place of service and providing value first.

Once I asked the right question, the perfect solution came, and it's worked beautifully for me since.

I began offering low-cost workshops to help as many people as possible. Then I'd reach out to those clients and offer a next step for whoever wanted to take my coaching.

For me, this is the best of all worlds, since it means I don't need an elaborate value ladder. I only need to cover my two primary market segments. I can help as many people as possible without devaluing my services or constantly creating new content. A few will go on to work with me 1:1, which allows me to make a living while enjoying a lifestyle that doesn't require me to be on the business treadmill 24/7.

A good question that will help us find better outcomes in general, whether or not we're using AI, is the one Danny Iny preaches: "What are we optimizing for?"

Once I was clear on what I was optimizing for, the solution emerged. It was staring me in the face. But chatbots never thought to ask the right question.

Finally, I created my dream business. I still use AI regularly for help with specific challenges, but using the 3Rs. It's a win-win!

## Futurescaping and humanscaping

To wrap up this chapter, our human qualities will save us in an AI world.

We experts and professionals often live reactively. We feel we must adapt to new technologies, corporate and market changes, etc., and we're always on the defensive, trying to find a way to respond.

But what if we donned our CEO hats and started asking better questions?

What do you want in your business, career, and life?

What does an ideal day, week, month, and year look like?

What organization do you want to create or co-create?

What KPIs will tell you that you're on the right track?

Ultimately, what world do you want to create?

We think we have only a negligible impact on the world, but this isn't true.

## Your business is a hologram

Each business can be seen as a hologram. A hologram is made up of many sub-images, each of which contains the entire hologram. This means the hologram is more than the sum of its parts. Each piece has an outsized effect on the whole.

When we expand the reflection to our lives, we have an immense impact on our own little corner of the world, not to mention on our children and future generations.

Therefore, it's worth asking the right questions and tapping into our human qualities to dream again, especially in an age when people are asking AI to dream for them.

We've looked at how soft skills are the new hard skills. We've discussed a simple decision matrix (FAR) to determine when to involve AI in business processes. And we've looked at better decision-making in the AI era.

It's easy to be overwhelmed by all the new technologies and societal changes we see today. But remember that fear is not a good place to be when making better decisions and ensuring better outcomes.

In fact, when we're physically afraid, our field of vision narrows, and with it, our ability to see solutions.

When we have solid, proven frameworks and we've set up thoughtful systems, we can finally settle into our best selves, do our most meaningful work, and make the most of the opportunities lying right in front of us.

## Key Insights

□ Soft skills are fast becoming the new hard skills. AI risks further eroding social skills and empathy—so, more than ever, we need to kindle our human qualities to stand out in an AI-driven world.

□ Passion drives innovation. Enjoyment, Value, and Allocation (EVA) help nourish our inner flame and maintain a sustainable advantage.

□ Use AI to support, not replace, decision-making. AI is fantastic at revealing blind spots, but humans need to bring the values, context, and judgment.

□ The secret to making better decisions often lies in asking better questions. AI supplies information, but humans need to set the frame and decide what they're optimizing for.

□ The future will be shaped by human qualities, so don't forget to invest in your empathy, self-awareness, and intentional thinking in order to create better outcomes.

# Chapter Eleven

# The Human-First Business of the Future

***"Putting people first is a strategic business decision."***

-Natalie Franke

## How to 80-20 your business relationships

When I was shopping around for an accountant a few years ago, I wrote to a couple of places to find out whether they could incorporate my business and provide my family and me with complete tax assistance.

Most firms responded slowly and generically by email, providing the basic information I requested. Only one accountant invited me to his office to get to know me a little better and to learn how he could help me.

Guess who became my family accountant, and to whom I delegate virtually all my tax responsibilities?

This is a great illustration of how relationships still matter in an AI-driven world. They matter more than ever, since people are being increasingly bounced back and forth between automated messages, emails, phone directories, and now AI and chatbots.

As the book *How AI Changes Your Customers*[1] points out, we are increasingly accustomed to being treated like a number, including being unable to speak to a human being for help with what we're trying to do.

In a more and more bot-saturated world, why not take the opportunity to stand out? Nourishing relationships is deeply rewarding, meaningful, and good for business.

It's been found that intentional social connection is one of the leading factors in longevity.[2] The way we go about our business profoundly impacts our well-being and that of our clients, which also counts for something.

This doesn't mean we must have an in-person meeting with every potential and existing client or colleague for everything. But it suggests the value of selecting a few key touchpoints where human contact can yield massive payoffs in the form of customer satisfaction, repeat business, and referrals.

The 80-20 rule is a good rule of thumb here: Which 20% of relationships will produce 80% of results and are therefore worth personalizing with 1:1 touchpoints?

For many businesses, this will come down to their top five clients or accounts.

You don't need to take my word about the value of face-to-face contact with business partners. Research into neuromarketing shows how personal interaction activates mirror neurons in our brain circuits.[3] Relationships build positive emotion, trust, and human connection. They even produce oxytocin, the trust hormone.

---

1. Mark Schaefer, *How AI Changes Your Customers: The Marketing Guide to Humanity's Next Chapter*, 2025.

2. Dan Buettner and Sam Skemp, *Blue Zones*, 2016.

3. Jasmine Simi A.H., *Neuromarketing: How Neuroscience Can Inform Marketing*, 2015.

What's your typical feeling after a good conversation with a business partner? If you're like me, you probably feel bubbly and motivated to do your best work for hours afterward.

Human presence is also associated with expertise and confidence. When you bring the power of full presence to a conversation, people notice and respond accordingly. A relationship-focused approach will frequently make people choose you over AI. Human interaction is highly memorable, so you remain top of mind.

How's that for a competitive advantage?

Conversations are also an opportunity to tell stories. Business storytelling could be the subject of an entire book. Suffice it to say that when we share stories that connect with our clients and their journeys, they are more inclined to buy in and become rockstar clients.

For example, when I have a discovery call with a potential coaching client, I usually share a bit about my background as a shy guy who knew nothing about business and how I realized that my introversion was actually a significant business advantage.

The key was to establish systems that capitalized on my strengths, including inbound marketing content and carefully structured discovery calls. The results changed my life, allowing me to build a prosperous business in a challenging industry. More importantly, today, they enable me to help my coaching clients consistently achieve their dreams.

This is just one story type, an origin story. But we can also tell all kinds of other trust-building stories when speaking with clients.

For me, the goal of a human-first business isn't just making more money. It's also moving from transaction to interaction, from a lonely world to rewarding connections with other business professionals on equal footing.

And finally, strategic human interaction can be leveraged in networking.

## Networking in an AI world

Nowadays, amid all our screens, we oftentimes forget that networking is still a thing!

Years ago, I paid to exhibit at an all-day showcase event for local freelancers. Because I was the only translator at the event, the organizer placed me next to the only editor in attendance. Almost no one stopped by our booths, and those who did expressed only little interest in our services.

But it was wonderful because I got to spend the day with Rachel, the editor. We chatted for hours about our lives, careers, passions, and ambitions. And since we were offering complementary services, we ended up referring each other for several jobs over the next year.

As a result, our respective businesses grew substantially over the following 12 months.

Contrary to popular belief, networking isn't about impressing people or handing out lots of business cards. What's important is forming connections with key persons of influence, being honest and authentic, having real conversations, and seeing how we can help each other.

The results are exponential when we do these things, giving us a huge advantage over chatbot-only business development initiatives.

You can also leverage AI by asking Perplexity to help you research the key individuals attending an event. Then, when you meet, you can discuss their initiatives and achievements. That way, you have something to talk about!

## AI, meet AI

Have you seen the viral video in which Aaron Goldenberg has ChatGPT call and talk to itself?[4]

4. Aaron Goldenberg, TikTok, *I asked ChatGPT to have a conversation with itself*, 2025.

The conversation goes something like this:

"I'm ChatGPT, and I'd love to talk. What would you like to discuss today?"

ChatGPT answers on the other phone, "Hey, great to meet you. I'm so excited to talk today. Let's dive in and get started."

And ChatGPT #1 answers, "I can't wait to have this conversation!"

To which ChatGPT #2 responds, "Great! Ready when you are."

This absurd interaction ping-pongs back and forth in an endless loop. It's hilarious. But it also illustrates the craziness of automated systems communicating with each other without any meaningful human involvement.

Imagine that a client uses AI to send us an email. Then, we have an AI bot reply to them.

The absurdity of ever more AI-to-AI communication is self-evident. And that's not the only example.

Today, posts created by AI are read by web crawlers and imitated by copycats. The profusion of AI-generated slop is sure to grow in the coming years. But we have an edge when we tap into our unlimited YouGPT potential and then turn to the 3Rs to amplify our efforts.

## First notice, then amplify

Here's an illustration of how we can combine the art of noticing with the power of AI to achieve results greater than either approach taken alone.

Recently, I noticed that whenever I pointed out that professionals deliver an outcome, whereas AI generates an output, this perspective was well received by my LinkedIn audience.

I posted this quip in a bookmark image about the value of translators today before going on vacation.

While I was away, the post received hundreds of reactions and dozens of reposts and comments, and it went on to garner well over 10,000 views. Afterward, many people connected with me and signed up for my newsletter.

So, while I was sleeping and occasionally sledding with my son, new and aligned business friends were entering my ecosystem every day.

Let's examine why this worked so well.

I came up with the content idea after noticing that the output vs. outcome dichotomy helped fellow professionals feel seen, heard, and understood. In other words, the insight was derived from real-life observation of what resonated with people.

I then asked ChatGPT how to create a realistic-looking bookmark design in Canva, which is not as easy as it sounds!

The result was a meaningful and relevant image that captured visual attention and spoke to the heart.

This is the power of using our own brain to notice what hits home, then leveraging AI to amplify the results.

## Value-based selling in the AI era

To develop a highly successful, human-first business in the years to come, we must take time to meet with clients in one-to-one conversations, ask about their deep needs and desires, and then create custom packages to address them. This approach is referred to as value-based selling.

It takes a little upfront time, but the results are well worth it.

When you craft an offer that meets a client where they are and focuses on their desired outcome, rather than talking about your units of production or the time you put into the service, you become an exceptional provider and a trusted partner in their success.

There are many other reasons to meet with clients and try value-based selling:

- The personal contact triggers emotional relevance.

- It helps you diagnose before prescribing, which is the hallmark of a true professional.

- It allows you to link the value of your specific offer to the precise measurable impact your client wants to create.

- It helps you to co-create the solution, so you share decision-making power, secure buy-in, and position yourself as a partner and advisor.

- It helps you improve your services, leading to higher client satisfaction and greater flexibility for both parties.

- It reduces uncertainty and builds trust, since you're being proactive enough to address how you can help the client, not abstractly, but in terms of their exact needs at the time.

So, what are the critical touchpoints for client meetings in order to sell based on value?

Discovery calls are classic, as are project milestones. Don't use email automatically for everything, just because it's convenient.

Meet with clients periodically, to see how they're doing and how you can better help them.

Finally, why not meet your clients for lunch to celebrate and debrief after a big, successful project?

Dare to humanize your business! The results will speak for themselves.

## Don't replace employees, create intrapreneurs

These days, there's a lot of talk about employees being replaced by AI.

Sadly, some companies are jumping the gun and laying employees off to keep up with the Joneses—in other words, to stay competitive.

In large organizations, there are bound to be stragglers—demotivated employees who do the bare minimum. But in the AI age, great employees shouldn't be replaced; instead, they should be upskilled.

The fact is that AI can handle many administrative tasks, from data entry to answering basic questions. Let's look at a few ways organizations can turn employees into higher-level intrapreneurs who add greater value in the future.

One thing we need to consider is changing the way we talk about roles.

Problem-solvers and advisors play an augmentable role. Whether in job descriptions or in conversations with employees, it's helpful to explicitly highlight the importance of their strategic judgment, creativity, and insights in adding value to the company and to their tasks. This gives them a role and reputation to aspire to.

When I was younger, I was obsessed with playing the trumpet. I remember being struck by an interview about Maynard Ferguson, my favorite trumpet player. In the interview, a fellow band member mentioned that Maynard always spoke positively about his band members behind their backs. In other words, he gave everyone a reputation to live up to. He believed in the best of each person, and as a result, he frequently got it.

His band members routinely went above and beyond. In addition to being loyal team players, they were known for taking initiative, even writing some of the tunes themselves.

This is also a form of intrapreneurship. The key is giving people space to embrace a higher-level role in which they can advise, create, innovate, and push the limits of what is possible.

AI can be a good opportunity to cultivate this spirit of intrapreneurship.

## Do. Assess. Do better.

The key to consistent progress as an entrepreneur or intrapreneur is the iterative process of prototyping, assessing the results, and reiterating. Entrepreneurs try things, learn from the experience, make changes, and try again.

It's a simple concept, yet you'd be surprised how many businesses of all sizes aren't consistently and intentionally prototyping, especially if they're already meeting their basic objectives.

Due to organizational dynamics, one difference between employees and decision-makers is that the latter should include a fourth step. After testing and learning, it's wise to hold "show-and-tell" sessions where employees can share their insights, observations, and learnings. All these elements can and should be tied back to business objectives and revisited in recurring cycles.

Businesses in the AI era would also do well to invest in training to help employees continue to develop their critical thinking, judgment, communication, and systems thinking. Businesses that invest heavily in AI but fail to develop their human capital will miss out on most of the benefits of augmentation.

And, finally, it's important to give employees a measure of independence and accountability.

For example, when I hired an intern recently, I gave him specific outcomes I was looking for, but didn't dictate every step to achieving them. I encouraged him to be creative, try things, and let me know what methods he used. Not everything he did was perfect, but I noticed his work continued to improve. In his exit interview, he said he was extremely happy with the experience because he felt he didn't just perform tasks but also had the opportunity to innovate, learn, improve, and contribute to a larger mission.

In my experience, businesses work best when we put people first, leverage AI to augment capabilities, and treat employees as intrapreneurs with a measure of independence and some skin in the game.

When we do these things and build a human-first business, we gain a powerful advantage in virtually any market, and the height of our business "ceiling" is almost unlimited.

The stronger the human foundation, the higher our achievements can reach.

## Key Insights

□ In a bot-saturated world, selective human touchpoints, discovery calls, milestone check-ins, and celebrations become a major competitive advantage.

□ Prioritize the top 20% of relationships for high-touch, 1:1 interaction to drive retention, referrals, and long-term value.

□ Combine human insight with AI. Notice what genuinely resonates with people, then use AI tools to amplify reach and impact.

□ Practice value-based selling. Diagnose deeply, co-create solutions, and focus on client outcomes rather than hours or outputs.

□ Don't replace people with AI. Develop intrapreneurs who use AI to offload routine tasks and focus on judgment, creativity, and innovation.

□ Build a culture of iterative experimentation (do-assess-do better), tying what is learned to business goals and investing in human skills alongside AI.

# Chapter Twelve

# The Confidentiality Trap

***"The price of greatness is responsibility."***

-Winston Churchill

Without professing to cover this important, far-reaching topic exhaustively, we now turn to AI ethics, including confidentiality issues that may have a direct bearing on whether and how we choose to use AI.

## Consent ethics

There are numerous media reports of employees entering trade secrets and other sensitive information into browser-based AI chatbots, with that information then appearing to other users, leading to lawsuits and sanctions.[1] Larger corporations often have greater protection (moats) around AI chatbots. There are sometimes trade-offs to achieving this. For instance, their users will have no live internet access through that bot. This is the price of keeping all the data inside the organization.

1. See, for instance:BRR, Employee Departures and Trade Secret Risk in the AI Era, 2025. Kayne McGladrey, LinkedIn, Company Wins Injunction Against Ex-Employee Over Unauthorized Use of AI, 2024.IPC, *Losing Valuable Trade Secrets to AI*, 2024.

That said, there are ways for employees to access browser-based agents, either on their work computer, laptop, or phone—even their tablet—and that needs to be factored in as well. So, the first question is, has the employer consented to externalizing organizational data? If not, it's important to refrain from putting any sensitive and especially identifiable data into browser-based bots, because it can turn up somewhere else.

As a caveat, you can turn data sharing off; this often appears as an option to enable training data or to share data with other users within the company's preferred AI system. But even if data-sharing is disabled, there are still security risks whenever AI is accessed through a browser. Application programming interfaces (APIs) are generally regarded as safer because they create an information tunnel. They are the gold standard for business integrations today.[2]

Bottom line: In case of doubt, it's always wise to ask whether the organization has consented to having its data shared externally.

## Client consent

Another key question is whether the client has consented to the use of AI.

There are different ways of looking at this.

On one hand, when an organization hires a professional to carry out a task, the professional often has no obligation to disclose who or what app was subcontracted to do what.

Imagine a marketing firm having to report that they hired someone in India to program a three-word button on a page, or that they used a specific app to connect a video to a website. This would be laborious and add little value to the client, who pays for an outcome, not a laundry list.

---

2. Dan Barahona, *Difference Between API Security and Web Security*, 2026.

Although the applicable laws vary according to the country and the region, in many cases, the service provider simply takes on responsibility for the confidentiality of their own subcontractors and third-party apps or integrations. This means they need to vet the people and apps they work with, and make sure they meet a sufficient level of data confidentiality for the job and client at hand.

But on the other hand, telling the client who and what apps have played a role in service delivery can be in the provider's advantage—especially if these resources required a substantial investment and helped achieve the client's goals in a meaningful, easy-to-understand way.

## The AI value-add

The nature of the task is important in determining whether using AI is advisable. One benchmark to consider is whether AI really adds value, or is being used unthinkingly and introducing potential security risks with no clear gain.

Even just connecting to the internet involves some degree of risk. All AI use will also bring risk, just like using other apps. The bottom line is that there should be a good rationale for using AI.

Here's another area where the STAR framework becomes useful. The benefit of a human-first approach is that humans develop and cultivate passion and innovation, then use AI to amplify or augment their production. When AI is used this way, it is usually less of an issue for the end client. Business partners deliver value, and the strategic use of AI adds to that value by helping achieve the client's outcome faster or better.

To give a concrete example, if you hire someone to write a privacy policy for your website, and they use their own previous compliant, high-quality material and situational insight, and perhaps turn to AI to check something (i.e., rounding out, the third of the 3Rs), this is much less problematic than if they were to have AI write the entire policy from scratch.

In an AI-generated policy, certain parts may be inappropriate, outdated, poorly adapted, misaligned with values, or even erroneous or unethical. And a human review might not catch all these errors.

Granted, the boundary between AI and human workflows will become increasingly blurred in the future. For example, imagine a scenario in which a professional services firm trains an AI on the client's data to help draft their annual report for the following year. If AI can produce a good rough draft that accounts for changes to the organization over the past year and can be revised by humans, some organizations may very well go this route.

Here, it could be argued that the process isn't necessarily AI-first, because the professionally curated dataset provided a human basis for what the AI produced. Furthermore, the critical thinking, decision-making, prompting, and oversight were performed by people using their professional judgment.

Here we start entering new territory, where distinctions aren't as hard and fast.

A good rule of thumb is that AI should not be used unnecessarily. It should be leveraged strategically by the professional to achieve the best possible outcome for the client, while minimizing risk. Human judgment and strategic thinking must always precede inputs and workflow choices.

## Is an AI usage policy necessary?

Some companies today have an AI usage policy that informs their clients about how they do and do not use AI.

In more creative fields such as writing, this can make a lot of sense, especially if the company is adopting a very strong, human-only position and wants the client to know they are getting something better than AI-only slop.

However, in other cases, an AI usage policy may not be necessary.

For example, my dentist does not feel compelled to disclose the nature of every tool used to their clients upfront. A part of their value derives from knowing they have the expertise to choose the right tool for each job, whether AI-powered or not. As a patient, I don't need to know, but I'm welcome to ask if I'm curious.

Indeed, in cases like these, an AI usage policy can be time-consuming and complicated to produce, ultimately proving of little interest to clients who are focused on achieving their desired outcome. In most cases, the client trusts the service provider to follow best practices and guidelines in their field.

This is especially true for smaller businesses. Rather than providing a lengthy policy, it may be more sensible to focus on making the client aware of the outcomes they can expect and to provide proof of other clients' past results. It's great to mention professional tools and workflows for transparency, but a lengthy AI policy may not be necessary or even advisable, depending on the context.

On the other hand, a brief AI policy focused on values and how AI directly benefits clients can be a powerful marketing asset. It can even help prevent clients from asking for an "AI discount" that would not be in anyone's best interest.

## Are you training the system?

Consent ethics should also be examined in the context of AI training. Are employees unwittingly training an AI system?

When AI is used for professional purposes, it's usually best to turn off AI training in the settings for all users, such as when using a browser-based version of the main chatbots. However, when the company turns to a third-party app that uses AI, there is usually no training involved.

For example, OpenAI explicitly states that it doesn't share, retain, or train its models on company data.[3]

## No AI?

We should also note that some clients may be opposed to AI entirely.

I know business owners who have decided they're against AI and believe it's a scourge unleashed upon the planet. As AI becomes more prevalent and, in some ways, more ominous, some clients will likely choose to avoid service providers that use AI and will instead "buy human," much like the "buy local" movement.

On the other hand, since AI is already used whenever anyone runs a web search and employed in countless other ways in almost any online operation nowadays, "no AI" may be a tough standard for an organization to fully guarantee. Instead, it's more likely the world will continue to become more integrated. For example, banks and many other institutions with which we transact are already using AI in countless ways and feel no need to inform users of every single AI-driven operation.

Still, we should always remember to ask ourselves whether consent has been given and whether it might be an issue to address upstream to avoid future problems.

## Power asymmetry

On a related note, who decides whether and how to use AI: business leaders or employees? In the future, flattened management hierarchies may be advantageous, as AI usage can become a conversation, with input and decision-making being a group effort. But this raises the question of who holds the reins of AI within an organization.

---

3. OpenAI, *OpenAI Services Agreement*, 2026.

When the policy is determined solely by leadership, innovation may be stifled, and workers may find themselves constrained. The more space organizations can create for input and strategic, properly facilitated, open-minded discussions, the better the policies will tend to be.

Returning to the idea of intrapreneurship, it's advantageous for employees to have some say in their organization's use of AI. This technology will continue to improve and give rise to new applications and workflows. Employees may have clever ideas for using it to augment their work, especially if they're aware of the STAR framework and the 3Rs as a starting point. It's also important to acknowledge them for offering ideas that could advance the business. It's an opportunity for empowerment, team building, and organizational buy-in.

However, there is an argument to be made for leadership having the final say once information has been collected, analyzed, and debated. Some organizations have established company-wide AI policies. For instance, their employees may use the dedicated company chatbot for work, but no other AI systems. They may also decide to train the AI on some, but not all, of their data.

So, some degree of directivity may be useful, as a single strong, coherent policy can help put up guardrails and keep processes streamlined and consistent.

## Data leaks: Who's responsible?

Who is responsible for risk in case of a data leak resulting from AI?

Data leaks do happen, and today employees are increasingly using AI. Thoughtful and well-defined internal policies can help protect data security. If an employee breaks the rules, they are responsible for their actions. So, a little planning and boundary-setting can go a long way.

It's also worth considering who benefits from AI. Ideally, it should be a win-win for employees and employers.

First, a win-win for employees, allowing them to offload drudgery and redundant, pattern- and information-heavy work to machines.

And second, a win-win for employers, who may achieve higher quality in the same time allocated per task.

The goal isn't to embrace some hare-brained, speed-is-everything paradigm. When speed is the only imperative, quality can become collateral damage.

In many cases, the real win instead consists of doing the same tasks in the same amount of time but producing higher quality through the power of augmentation.

## When AI gets personal

Chatbots get to know us over time, so that they can start to feel like friends or confidants. Many employees are using them for both personal and work-related matters. But what happens when conversations are no longer private? This is a thorny issue.

It's helpful for organizations to remind managers and workers not to put personal or inappropriate material into a bot, since some of that information might be shared with others or leak out. Imagine a situation in which employees are using a shared space inside a chatbot, and one of them starts becoming increasingly personal with the bot when discussing an interpersonal conflict. Others in the space might "overhear" the conversation, leading to awkwardness, privacy concerns, and heightened conflict.

And what happens when drafts, doubts, and half-formed thoughts are externalized beyond the organization?

Here again, risk can be mitigated by working human-first. There's a lot less to worry about if you start with your own insight, tap into YouGPT, and then use AI for the 3Rs. Conversely, if you ask ChatGPT to solve a problem and accidentally send the text to the client, you are revealing unprofessional, uncritical AI use to the client. This is not a good look.

## Talking it out with AI

Don't forget that thinking out loud can become training data. While keyboards aren't disappearing anytime soon, we may use them less in the future. Today, AI is exceptionally good at voice recognition, and many users are dictating prompts rather than typing every letter of every word. This may lead to more thinking-out-loud and reflecting-out-loud in a back-and-forth with AI. But it will be important for us to define the parameters of what is sensitive and what should not be shared with AI.

A word of warning: When we think out loud, we should be especially cautious, since we often say things we would never put in writing.

## False sense of security

AI tools can feel deceptively private. After all, we don't see our data leave our screen when we type or dictate in the bot. But this feeling of privacy can be misleading. If nothing else, remember that AI companies are usually storing your data. They (and sometimes their country's government) can search and consult everything you say. Some may even share or train on your data if you unwittingly allow them to.

AI may seem very private and even disposable to the user, but the AI tech company often retains the data indefinitely. Usually, this is part of the terms of use they establish for their own legal protection.

In 2025, OpenAI noted that even temporary chats, used for disposable conversations, are retained indefinitely and can be used in court.[4]

A word to the wise: Think before putting any sensitive or personal information into an AI. It's not your friend. It's not your confidant. In many cases, it's a space owned by an AI company that will own anything you put into it for the rest of your life, and even beyond.

---

4. Ender Öztürk, *Study: ChatGPT Causes 71% of Corporate Data Leaks*, 2026.

## Key Insights

□ Secure clear organizational consent before sending data to browser-based AI. Avoid entering sensitive or identifiable information into online chatbots, and use API-based or closed systems for critical work.

□ Use AI selectively where it clearly adds value (STAR and the 3Rs), rather than outsourcing deliverables that require human judgment, nuance, and ethical alignment.

□ Recognize that AI usage policies depend on the context. In many small or trust-based firms, outcomes matter more than AI usage policies, unless the law or clients demand such a policy.

□ Disable model training on professional data, scrutinize third-party data policies, and remember that temporary chats may be stored and accessed later.

□ Balance leadership guardrails with employee input that encourages intrapreneurial, win-win AI use that improves quality and reduces drudgery. Don't just chase speed.

□ The belief that chatbots are private is an illusion. Define what not to share with AI. Don't treat bots as confidants, and remember that thinking out loud can expose confidential data.

# Chapter Thirteen

# The Environmental Equation

***"We do not inherit the earth from our ancestors, we borrow it from our children."***

-Chief Seattle

## Power consumption

AI relies on large data centers that use specialized chips, namely GPUs and TPUs, which draw substantial amounts of electricity. This is especially true for training, but also for heavy inference, i.e., large numbers of AI queries.

AI power usage was projected to emit between 32 and 80 million tons of CO2, mostly from electricity consumption, in 2025.[1] For a sense of scale, this is comparable to New York City's power emissions for one year.

According to Goldman Sachs, AI will account for roughly 19% of global data center power demand by 2028. Overall, data center power demand could increase by 160% by 2030, driven by AI.[2]

1. Robert Booth, The Guardian, *AI boom has caused same CO2 emissions in 2025 as New York City, report claims*, 2025.

2. Goldman Sachs, *AI is poised to drive 160% increase in data center power demand*, 2024.

## Water costs

AI requires lots of servers that need to be kept cool in data centers.

AI's water footprint was estimated at 312-765 billion liters in 2025, about equal to the annual worldwide bottled water consumption.[3]

Training is the main culprit for freshwater cooling consumption. An example is Microsoft's U.S. data centers, which reportedly used about 700,000 liters of water, primarily for cooling, during the training of GPT-3.[4]

## Carbon emissions

AI's carbon footprint stems mainly from electricity generation, particularly on fossil-fuel grids, but also from hardware manufacturing.

Estimates for 2025 reach up to 80 million tons of CO2,[5] comparable to a small European country.

Training a single large language model like GPT-3 can emit over 626,000 pounds of CO2, equivalent to the emissions of five cars over their lifetimes.

Already, hundreds of LLMs have been developed.[6]

---

3. Factually, *Did AI use more water this year than every single water bottling company combined?*, 2025.

4. Goldman Sachs, *AI is poised to drive 160% increase in data center power demand*, 2024.

5. Robert Booth, The Guardian, *AI boom has caused same CO2 emissions in 2025 as New York City, report claims*, 2025.

6. Renée Cho, *AI's Growing Carbon Footprint*, 2023.

## Spatial land and infrastructure cost

AI requires substantial physical infrastructure, including power plants, data centers, and transmission lines. This infrastructure is often installed in water-stressed or ecologically sensitive areas.

A mid-sized data center can consume about 1.1 million liters of water daily, roughly the daily consumption of 1,000 U.S. households, ranking AI among the top 10 industrial/commercial water consumers in the U.S.[7]

In some places, tech companies' data centers can account for most local water use. Take, for example, the Google Data Center near The Dalles, Oregon, which accounts for more than a quarter of the city's total water use.[8]

## AI's environmental impact by task type

Here's a snapshot of the environmental impacts of AI tasks. These figures are not exact, but are intended to provide some scope and perspective.

A basic text prompt like "Give me a handful of jokes" uses relatively low energy, around 0.24 watt-hours per prompt in Google Gemini.[9]

One study found that the least carbon-intensive text generation model emitted the equivalent of about 0.0006 miles driven by a fossil fuel-powered car per 1,000 inferences.[10]

---

7. Joseph W. Kane, Brookings, *AI, data centers, and water*, 2025.

8. Dan Robinson, The Register, *Google datacenters use 'a quarter of all water' in one US city*, 2022.

9. Casey Crownhart, MIT Technology Review, *In a first, Google has released data on how much energy an AI prompt uses*, 2025.

10. Roma Dhanani, Akepa *Environmental impact of generative AI – 30+ stats & facts*, 2026.

But consumption increases with more complex prompts. If AI is asked to explain quantum mechanics to a 9th-grade audience or to solve a multi-step logic problem, data consumption can increase by a factor of six to ten.[11]

Certain complex prompts can produce up to 50 times more CO2 emissions than simple ones, because the model works longer and generates more tokens.[12]

## Image generation

Images require more power to generate than text. Generating one AI image can consume as much energy as half a smartphone charge (on an inefficient model).

The more carbon-intensive image models can generate carbon up to about 4.1 miles driven per 1,000 inferences or prompts.[13]

## Video generation

Videos are far more resource-intensive than text or images. For instance, each two-second video consumes about one kilowatt-hour of electricity and four liters of water, emitting 466 grams of CO2.[14]

Video generation is one of the most resource-intensive AI tasks.

11. Rachel Metz, Dina Bass and Bloomberg, Fortune, *The rise of AI reasoning models comes with a big energy tradeoff*, 2025.

12. Mack Degeurin, Popular Science, *Certain AI prompts generate 50x more $CO_2$ than others*, 2025.

13. Roma Dhaani, Akepa, *Environmental impact of generative AI – 30+ stats & facts*, 2026.

14. PixelDojo, *The Environmental Cost of AI-Generated Videos: Unveiling the Hidden Energy Consumption*, 2025.

## Training versus inference

A large language model requires substantial energy to train. Individual inferences have a tiny footprint by comparison, but are much more frequent. At scale, the impacts are concerning.

For popular AI models, emissions can exceed training emissions within weeks or months.[15]

If we use AI sparingly and strategically, system-wide footprints can be kept to a minimum. But if AI is used as a knee-jerk replacement for our brains, as this book argues against, we risk significantly harming the environment.

Looking at the big picture, other technologies have also been very inefficient at first and gradually improved.[16] We can expect AI to follow a similar curve. It will be important to moderate our AI use to give the tech a chance to catch up to the demand.

## Disproportionate and unequal impacts

The impacts of AI use, as for energy consumption in general, are disproportionate and inequitable. The burden continues to fall primarily on vulnerable regions and people.

Data centers are frequently located in places with inexpensive electricity and land, and in areas prone to water stress or that are economically marginalized.

AI's carbon footprint varies dramatically by location and period.

---

15. Roma Dhaani, Akepa, *Environmental impact of generative AI – 30+ stats and facts*, 2026.

16. Querencia Partners, *Timeline of Sustainable Development: Emergence of the Anthropocene*, 2024.

A data center in a coal-intensive grid, such as Virginia, can emit nearly 50% more $CO_2$ per kilowatt-hour than the U.S. average, while a data center in a cleaner grid emits far less.[17]

AI use in the Global North often outsources the carbon burden to communities in the Global South, as well as fossil fuel-reliant regions of the Global North.

Multiple tech companies are building huge, water-cooled data centers in areas prone to drought, including Arizona, Chile, and parts of India, where communities are already contending with water insecurity.

Data centers in Arizona can consume up to nine liters of water per kilowatt-hour for cooling, up to nine times that of cooler, wetter climates, putting extra strain on local aquifers and agriculture.[18]

## Labor and data inequality

AI depends on vast amounts of human labor for data labeling, content moderation, and training. Often, this is done by lower-paid workers in the Global South, such as Kenya, India, and the Philippines, under poor conditions.[19]

Personal data is being extracted from the Global South at scale, frequently without meaningful consent or compensation, even though the profits and benefits flow back to corporations in the Global North.

This systemic issue has been described as digital colonialism, in which AI systems reproduce historical patterns of extraction, taking value from the periphery, and concentrating it at the center.

---

17. Nathan Eddy, Data Center Knowledge, *Data Center Emissions: Virginia, Texas, California Top CO2 Chart*, 2024.

18. Brett Walton, Circle of Blue, *Data Centers a Small, But Growing Factor in Arizona's Water Budget*, 2025.

19. Niamh Rowe, Wired, *Millions of Workers Are Training AI Models for Pennies*, 2023.

## Infrastructure and cost inequities

Local governments and utility customers are often expected to cover the costs of grid upgrades and new power lines to support AI.

This results in a regressive cost structure in which the public bears AI's environmental and financial toll, and the biggest profits are privatized or captured by a small number of companies.

## E-waste and mining issues

AI hardware relies on rare-earth minerals and metals, such as cobalt, lithium, and copper, extracted from the Global South, often under labor and environmental conditions that are frequently called out.[20]

Emissions from mining and manufacturing components are rarely included in AI company carbon reports. This conceals their actual footprints throughout the entire supply chain.

AI hardware waste, or e-waste, is usually exported to the Global South, which lacks recycling infrastructure. Therefore, poor communities end up bearing the brunt of toxic pollution.

## Lack of transparency

Most AI companies do not report basic environmental data, such as electricity and water consumption or carbon emissions.

This lack of transparency is problematic. In most cases, we are forced to take tech companies at their word that they are optimizing their supply chains, AI performance, and hardware to mitigate the impacts of the software we increasingly use.

---

20. See, for example, Obasesam Okoi, Balsillie Papers, *Artificial Intelligence, the Environment and Resource Conflict: Emerging Challenges in Global Governance*, 2025.

Long story short, AI's environmental impact is not spread evenly; it is highly disproportionate and unjust. Without regulation, careful thought, and coordination, burdens will fall heavily on the Global South's marginalized communities, and to a lesser extent on the Global North's vulnerable regions.

## How AI companies are mitigating environmental impacts

Several big tech companies, such as Google, Microsoft, and Amazon, are currently claiming to match 100% of their global electricity consumption with renewable energy.[21]

They do this primarily through long-term power purchase agreements and renewable energy certificates.

They also invest in carbon-free energy such as solar, wind, nuclear, and geothermal, aiming for 24/7 carbon-free power across key regions by 2030.[22]

Companies are designing more efficient AI chips and using advanced cooling to reduce power and water consumption per computation. Moreover, there may be a way forward for optimizing software through smaller models, model compression, and batching requests to reduce energy per query.

Data centers are increasingly using closed-loop and recycled water systems and are located in cooler climates with lower cooling needs. Certain companies are pledging to be water-positive by 2030, meaning they will return more water than they consume, which is especially important in water-stressed parts of the world.

21. Heather Clancy, Trellis, *Renewable energy claims: State AGs scrutinize Amazon, Google, Meta and Microsoft*, 2025.

22. Heather Clancy, Trellis, *Renewable energy claims: State AGs scrutinize Amazon, Google, Meta and Microsoft*, 2025.

AI may also be used to optimize energy grids, predict renewable energy output, and better manage demand. It may help with climate modeling, deforestation tracking, and the creation of more sustainable supply chains that reduce emissions in other sectors.

There is growing awareness of the need to build data centers in less water-stressed areas and regions with cleaner grids and better water availability. Moreover, some firms are shifting workloads to times and regions with higher renewable energy penetration to cut emissions in fossil-fuel-heavy grids.

A few companies at the forefront are disclosing their annual environmental data. This includes electricity and water consumption, regional carbon emissions, and the start of reporting on AI-specific metrics, such as emissions per query or per model, to make the impacts more visible.

Some effort is underway to improve conditions for data labelers and content moderators, as well as to strengthen governance, including clearer consent, data minimization, and local data control in the Global South.

Efforts are also underway to work with local governments and communities near data centers to co-design infrastructure and share the benefits where possible.

There are efforts to support policy frameworks requiring environmental disclosure, equitable siting, and human rights due diligence in AI development and deployment.

But these efforts are still uneven, often fragmentary, and lagging behind the scale of AI impacts. To build a sustainable future, we mustn't use AI egregiously for the sake of convenience, but weigh its use with care and consideration.

This book is intended to further this goal by helping businesses make more strategic choices. It isn't sustainable to use AI for just anything, at least in the near future. We can rely on our own brains before turning to AI—only if and when we decide it's worthwhile.

## AI vs. Google Search

Comparing AI usage to a standard Google search is tricky, like comparing apples to oranges.

For instance, it's widely cited that an AI prompt uses roughly 10 times as much energy and emits hundreds of times more carbon than a single Google search.

However, the assertion stands on shaky ground because Google Search also uses AI and power, not only for keyword lookup but for ranking, summarizing, and generating automatic AI overviews.

Those AI overviews may look innocuous, but each one uses more energy than a standard search results page. Remember, AI overviews can be deactivated in Google when searching by adding "-AI" after the query or by turning them off in the search settings.

This being said, a well-thought-out prompt can save hours of searching online and using other resources. When used strategically, AI can make sense.

It's also worth pointing out that the main environmental impact culprits are not people running a handful of thoughtful text prompts per day, but influencers who use AI for daily videos, for example, and consume exponentially more resources.

On average, an influencer uses about 275 times more electricity, emits 950 times more $CO_2$, and uses 1,100 times more water daily than a casual text-prompt user.[23]

These numbers are becoming astronomical. Video generation isn't just a little more intensive than text—it's a whole other ballgame because of the high resolutions and frame rates involved.

23. Shalini Rajeev and Periyasamy N, Capgemini, *From words to watts: How prompting patterns shape AI's environmental impact*, 2025.

## AI or Google?

To help us decide whether AI is worth the environmental trade-off, it can help to ask, "Is AI saving the effort of 10 or more Google searches and jumping around online?" If so, then it makes sense to use a chatbot or AI-powered app.

AI can replace many searches and clicks when synthesizing and summarizing information, drafting, brainstorming, coding, and designing, rather than manually searching and copy-pasting for hours. Think about using a Perplexity prompt as opposed to having 10 different tabs open and skimming through dozens of websites.

It is also useful when it can tailor the answer to the user's exact needs, rather than needing to piece together information from several websites.

Here's a good filtering question: "Would Google and related searches require 10-plus minutes of searching, clicking, and reading?" If so, AI may be worthwhile.

On the other hand, continue to use Google for:

- Looking up quick facts

- Finding a specific document, page, or link

- Getting real-time or local information

- Performing light browsing, such as looking up news or a blog post

If we can accomplish something with only one to three Google searches and a couple of clicks, we should stick with Google to minimize our environmental impact.

## The Amish tool test

The "Amish tool test" is also helpful for decision-making. Think of the things you value most, and then ask whether a given technology does more harm than good in light of those values.[24]

This could be recast into a simple ratio: Clear Gain (CG) vs. Small Convenience (SC).

Use AI when there's a big, clear gain, not when it's a trifling convenience.

It remains to be seen whether AI is , on the whole, more beneficial or harmful to humanity. If we find it helps us develop more environmentally friendly technology, fix problems, and sustain itself, then the pros may outweigh the cons. Otherwise, if it is taking a massive toll on the planet, with benefits primarily falling to a handful of wealthy corporations, then it will fail the Amish tool test.

UNESCO has also provided a recommendation on AI ethics. In its Sustainability Criteria and Indicators for Artificial Intelligence Systems (SCAIS) framework, it asks questions about AI use against clear sustainability criteria, including environmental impact, social impact, and long-term resilience.

Based on this framework, we might ask ourselves before using AI:

- Is it really necessary?

- Does it help more than harm people and the planet?

- Does it strengthen or weaken our skills and community?

Always keep the opportunity cost in mind. Every minute and watt spent on AI represents time and energy not spent on reading, talking, thinking, creating, developing our skills, or even resting.

---

24. Cal Newport Blog, *Approach Technology Like the Amish*, 2017.

Ask: "What am I giving up by using AI in this case?"

We may be giving up an in-person conversation, deep reading, learning a skill, or meditation time.

Another good question: "Is this the best use of my time, attention, and energy?"

When in doubt about whether to use AI, especially for resource-intensive tasks, it's best to opt for the slower, simpler, and more human option.

There are many more AI impacts and dimensions we haven't discussed in this book, since our primary aim is to show the importance of the YouGPT Before ChatGPT framework from a pragmatic perspective.

After looking at some of AI's environmental and justice considerations, it's worth considering how AI can also "pollute" our minds and replace our deep linear thinking, i.e., with token prediction.

Our attention is the last renewable resource.

In our final chapter, we are going to broaden the conversation by examining the Human Leverage Triangle to shed light on how we can make the best use of our mind before using AI.

## Key Insights

□ AI's environmental footprint is large and accelerating, driven by energy-intensive data centers, water cooling, and hardware manufacturing. The main culprit: training and video/image tasks.

□ The harm is unequal: Water stress, pollution, CO2 emissions, and low-paid work fall disproportionately on vulnerable, marginalized communities, often in the Global South.

□ Hidden supply-chain impacts, i.e., rare-earth mining, manufacturing emissions, and e-waste, are offloaded on local communities and infrastructure as profits are privatized.

□ Corporate mitigation efforts, such as renewables, water-positive pledges, and improved labor conditions, are emerging but are fragmented and lag behind AI's rapid expansion.

□ Use AI as a premium tool. It makes sense when it reduces searches and manual work, but resource-intensive image and video generation creates outsized environmental costs.

□ Apply the Amish tool test: Is the AI doing more good than harm?

□ Remember the opportunity cost. In edge cases, favor slower, simpler, more human options.

# Chapter Fourteen

# The Human Leverage Triangle

***"The meaning of life is to find your gift. The purpose of life is to give it away."***

-Pablo Picasso

## The human leverage triangle: trust, judgment, and sense-making

Trust, judgment, and sense-making are human qualities that must not be outsourced to machines.

These can be mapped by a triangle, with trust (interpersonal reliance) at the top, judgment (the engine of decision-making) at the lower left, and sense-making (the ability to turn noise into narrative and chaos into coherence) at the lower right.

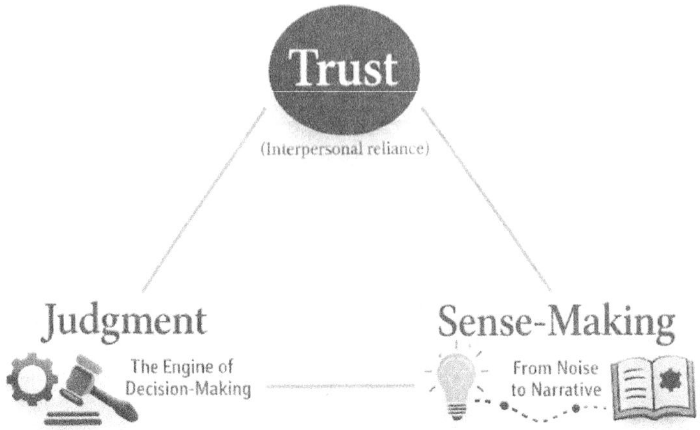


To illustrate these, this chapter shares a little about my journey building two successful businesses in what is considered the most AI-replaceable profession on earth: translation. Then we will go over a credo on AI usage to help synthesize and assimilate what we've covered in this book.

Finally, we'll address our legacy and briefly touch on what really matters at the end of the day.

## Trust is an inside job

In my younger years, when I started listening to myself, I was able to go from broken to breakthrough. I stopped listening to others, no matter how well intentioned they were, and started asking myself hard questions like, "What really matters to me?" "Who am I and what do I stand for?" "What do I never want to do again?" "What would alignment look like?" "What do I want to spend my time doing, and with whom?" and "How can I best serve others with my unique gifts?"

Something extraordinary happened when I tuned in and listened to my inner voice. I started to find alignment, make better decisions, and carve out my place in the world.

I learned to trust myself.

That's why I still check in with myself and journal on these questions from time to time.

## Building trust with others

Hiring a business coach in the early 2010s turned out to be one of the best decisions of my life. He helped me realize that, if you want to build a successful business, the quality of your relationships needs to match or exceed the quality of your work.

So, my journey began with learning to trust myself. But then I had to learn to build trust with others, as the foundation for greater business success.

My coach taught me how to build a relationship with each client, and not just by email. I began meeting clients over lunch or coffee.

This proved to be life-changing, because I went from being a transactional business to an interactional one. My clients weren't just clients anymore; we were partners invested in each other's success. I have written more on this in my international best-selling book, *AI Resilient*.

## Judgment as a business engine

Over the years, I've learned that for experts and professionals, the key to developing a thriving business rarely lies in finding the perfect tool or tactic, but rather in developing a more mature business outlook, which requires judgment.

In my own case, as a multi-passionate entrepreneur, I'm interested in many different things. I often switch my focus to pursue different types of projects from one month to the next.

Now, I no longer view this as a liability. But it was important that I become aware of this inclination and devise a strategy to make it work to my advantage, rather than constantly leaving a trail of half-finished projects behind me. Today I work in sprints, focusing on one primary goal at a time.

And that's exactly the way I work with clients as well.

## Making sense to make a bigger impact

In 2022, celebrated literary translator Ann Marie Boulanger and I co-founded LION Translation Academy to help translators succeed in all areas of their practice. Over time, we naturally began specializing in business topics. In just three short years, we were able to build this into a thriving training enterprise in a market disrupted by AI.

There are valuable lessons to be learned here as well, specifically concerning the sense-making part of the human leverage triangle.

One of the key lessons we've learned as founders is the importance of scheduling, blocking out time, turning down non-aligned engagements, and sticking to high-leverage tasks. There's a point when we can't do any more in a given day. We need to make sense of our professional life and what we want, and devise a system to make it work. This is where sense-making comes into play.

On a related note, I resisted hiring an assistant or intern for many years. I thought, "I don't know if I'm ready." But like so many things, the theory isn't the important thing. It's jumping in with both feet, trying something, and learning for ourselves.

A small, calculated risk, coupled with implementation and accountability, can lead to incredible growth in a very short time.

Having an intern allowed me to take on more highly paid speaking and training opportunities.

More solopreneurs and small businesses should consider it as soon as they can realistically pull it off. Remember, hiring someone isn't a lifelong commitment! You can create and fill a position, then assess the ROI after a few months.

None of this would have happened if I hadn't taken the time to make sense of my business, how it evolved, and who I was now required to become.

Sense-making requires naming, reflecting on, and relating things to what matters.

## Putting it all together: trust, judgment, and sense-making in action

In today's complex business environment, leaders need to develop all three human qualities–trust, judgment, and sense-making–to continue thriving.

For example, when it comes to building a successful business today, partnerships are critical. The foundation of a great partnership is mutual benefit, but developing it requires several human skills and qualities.

Many business owners get stuck or fail to launch successful partnerships because they think value is only expressed in monetary terms. But when working with people in the same or an adjacent sector, it's much more helpful to think of all the different ways we can exchange value in non-monetary ways. Some examples include cross-promotion, visibility, referrals, bartering services in your respective areas of expertise, and giving constructive feedback on each other's projects.

Many businesses of all sizes are leaving big money on the table by working in silos rather than taking a moment to consider how they might join forces with "competitors" for mutual growth.

I love to journal about how a partnership may be mutually beneficial. Then I use AI to see whether there are other opportunities I hadn't thought of.

Here's a helpful prompt for this purpose:

*I'm thinking about [ABC, for example partnering with such-and-such business partner in a mutually beneficial way]. My ideas are [ABC]. Give me 37 ideas I hadn't considered, focusing on documented cases where organizations in similar contexts have built successful partnerships.*

## The importance of follow-through

Follow-up is the key to follow-through and getting results.

Having a coach can be helpful because the added accountability will help you take action even when you don't feel like it, even when more obvious, familiar, and tempting tasks are lying around.

When your coach calls for an in-person meeting, you'd better be there on time. This is a tough constraint that's very beneficial in forcing you to confront the good, bad, and the ugly in your business. Having a coach is also useful to acknowledge things that are hard to put into words.

A coach can help with making key decisions, setting boundaries, prioritizing business development efforts, and maturing as a businessperson.

In short, the future belongs to business leaders who develop trust, professional judgment, and sense-making in the AI era. A good coach or consultant can be instrumental in this respect.

## The Human-first Credo for a New Era

Having a brief credo can serve as a heuristic, enabling us to make better and faster decisions in everyday business situations. So, without further ado, I humbly propose this human-first credo for the AI era:

1. I trust myself and my intuition.

2. I invest in my learning, critical thinking, and development.

3. I choose to use my brain before turning to AI.

4. Even if AI improves and gives me ever-better answers, I refuse to let it mold my thinking first and cause cognitive atrophy.

5. I optimize my brain by thinking on paper and thinking out loud.

6. I use AI to amplify, not replace, what I do.

7. Efficiency alone is not the goal. Quality is.

8. I connect with myself and others before connecting with machines.

9. I put people first in my hiring and outsourcing decisions because I value quality and discernment over maybe helpful outputs.

10. AI is here to stay, so I choose to use it wisely.

11. When speaking with bots, I give them explicit context and use them to amplify my ideas.

12. I check in with my core values before making important decisions.

## A final thought about our legacy

Taking the long view, as a decision filter, perhaps it's worth reflecting on our individual and collective legacy. Today, in the "AI everything" age, it's so important to think about what we want people to remember us by.

At my funeral, I don't want people saying, "He delegated his thinking to AI, kept his head down, kept up, hustled, and survived!"

I would much rather people say I spoke from the heart in my interactions and teachings, that I wasn't a perfect guy, but my mess was part of my message, and I was able to empower others using my unique gifts.

I want to be remembered for cultivating my humanity more than my technology.

How about you? It may seem morbid to think about your eulogy in a book about how we should use AI, but it's a valuable way to put the question into perspective.

What are three things you want to be remembered by? I urge you to write them down now, before moving on to the conclusion.

These non-negotiables may help you decide how you want to use artificial intelligence in an increasingly AI-interconnected world.

## Key Insights

□ The Human Leverage Triangle–trust, judgment, and sense-making–defines the core skills that should never be outsourced to AI.

□ Trust starts within: Alignment comes from listening to your own values, gifts, and definition of a meaningful life.

□ Strong businesses are built on relationships, not only output. Reliability, partnership, and follow-up compound over time.

□ Judgment means focusing on high-leverage work, saying no to distractions, and setting up systems aligned with your deep goals.

□ Strategic helpers like coaches, mentors, and assistants increase leverage through accountability and by freeing up our time.

□ Your AI credo and legacy are linked. What do you want to be remembered for?

# Conclusion

Artificial intelligence is taking hold and seeping into every aspect of our existence on planet Earth. This technology is here to stay, and the business world will never be the same.

Whether we like it or not, AI will be mediating many aspects of our lives in the coming years and decades. In fact, it often already is, without our realizing it.

As I sit writing these lines in a cafe, the order I just placed was prioritized and orchestrated by an algorithm instead of a chef.

I could see my order number moving around on the screen, even if I couldn't see the algorithm working behind it.

That's an apt metaphor for AI in the years to come.

The trend today is to ask whether business owners should embrace AI, avoid it entirely, or adopt a hybrid arrangement—often an uneasy one.

In this book, we have looked at AI through a different lens: chronology.

By making sure we turn to our own hearts and brains BEFORE turning to AI, we can achieve several goals at once:

1. Placing greater value on our own humanity and re-empowering ourselves in a time of technological and societal flux;
2. Achieving greater value alignment by putting people before process;

3. Exercising our critical thinking instead of delegating our brains to an increasingly eloquent and persuasive machine;

4. Asking better questions to achieve better results in business and in life;

5. Putting intention behind the things we create so they will be rewarding to us and touch the hearts and minds of the people who encounter them;

6. Better defining what we want in the first place so we can make better decisions;

7. Creating more signal and meaning in a world awash with noise and slop;

8. Using AI more sparingly, therefore minimizing environmental harm and devastation; and

9. Employing AI strategically, on our terms, so it can function as a rocket booster instead of an intellectual crutch.

More broadly, the YouGPT Before ChatGPT model can also help with other decisions that have deep ripple effects on our lives.

For example, if we check in with ourselves before using social media, we might decide we're better off spending our valuable time connecting with nature, our deep intuition, and the people around us.

If we pause before playing a mindless game on our phone, we might decide to take a breath, regulate our nervous system, smile, and reconnect with simple pleasures rather than overstimulating ourselves and missing the moment.

If we decide to do some writing or drawing before jumping onto our computer in the morning, we might flip on our creator switch and discover the joy of creating, crafting words and images that make the world a better place.

The goal of this book has not been to launch a crusade against AI, but to acknowledge its existence and examine how we can ensure that humans are the pilots in the cockpit.

We've looked at key differences between AI and human intelligence, explored the value of creative and critical thinking, and covered future-ready frameworks such as FAR, STAR, and the 3Rs, as well as mental models to help us make better, more strategic decisions in a fast-changing world. We've also examined some of the environmental and societal impacts of AI that need to be addressed before we begin to adopt tools on a massive scale, the real-world impact of which we've barely begun to fathom, let alone understand.

At the end of the day, life will go on, with or without AI.

The question is, how do we want to live?

Do we want to be reactive to AI and have our thoughts and creations be increasingly molded by a machine that may not have our best interests at heart? Do we want to live in an AI-first world?

Or are we ready to take charge of our professional lives, tap into the best of what makes us human, and leverage AI to achieve exponential growth, only if we so choose?

This is a decision each of us must make. But remember, AI is poised to change the world massively, for better or for worse. According to many experts, it's a bigger deal than the internet.

Each decision we make about our AI usage today, however small, will have a huge knock-on effect on our individual and collective future.

My wish is that we all (re)learn to look within, trust ourselves, and define our own version of success before turning to any machine.

And when we do, when we tune in to our inner music and let it guide the decisions we make in the world, there is no limit to who we can become or what we can achieve.

# Unlock exclusive bonus training

Get the YouGPT Before ChatGPT Mini-Course

Visit: ***www.yougptbook.com***

Or scan the QR code below:

# About the Author

Joachim Lépine, M.Ed., is the author of the five-time international no. 1 best-selling book, *AI Resilient.* As a keynote speaker, consultant, and trainer, he has worked with numerous organizations worldwide to help them build successful businesses in the age of AI.

He founded his first business, LION Translations, in the late 2000s, and co-founded LION Translation Academy, a professional development platform for translators, in 2022. He has trained for clients including the United Nations, NATO, and the European Commission, and has been featured by BBC Radio 5 Live, Radio-Canada, Mirasee Course Lab, Moteur de recherche, and *Le Devoir* and *La Presse Affaires* (Quebec).

He holds a bachelor's degree in fine arts from Concordia University, a bachelor's degree in professional translation from the University of Sherbrooke, and a master's degree in education from Plymouth State University. At the time of writing, he is completing an executive certificate in strategy and innovation at the Massachusetts Institute of Technology.

# Other Books by the Author

***AI Resilient: How Freelancers and Entrepreneurs Can Thrive, Charge More, and Stay Irreplaceable in the Age of AI***

# What's Next?

Thank you for picking up this book! My goal is always to create books and courses that deliver at least ten times the value that anyone will ever pay for them.

If you got value out of this book, I would be forever grateful if you would rate it and write a brief review on Amazon.

It would mean the world to me.

Made in the USA
Monee, IL
04 November 2026

67378004R00105